And That Was the Last Time
I Saw My Family

A Memoir in Essays

by Ina Teich

JewishGen

מרכז עולמי לגנאלוגיה יהודית

The Global Home for Jewish Genealogy

A Publication of JewishGen
Edmond J. Safra Plaza, 36 Battery Place, New York, NY
10280
646.494.2972 | info@JewishGen.org | www.jewishgen.org

JewishGen is the Genealogical Research Division of the
Museum of Jewish Heritage – A Living Memorial to the
Holocaust

MUSEUM OF
JEWISH HERITAGE
A LIVING MEMORIAL
TO THE HOLOCAUST

b

And That Was the Last Time I Saw My Family
A Memoir in Essays

Author: Ina Teich

Cover Design: Rachel Kolokoff Hopper

Library of Congress Control Number (LCCN): 2024939767

ISBN: 978-1-954176-26-3 (Hard cover: 132 pages, alk. paper)

About JewishGen.org

JewishGen, is a Genealogical Research Division of the Museum of Jewish Heritage - A Living Memorial to the Holocaust, serves as the global home for Jewish genealogy.

Featuring unparalleled access to 30+ million records, it offers unique search tools, along with opportunities for researchers to connect with others who share similar interests. Award winning resources such as the Family Finder, Discussion Groups, and ViewMate, are relied upon by thousands each day.

In addition, JewishGen's extensive informational, educational and historical offerings, such as the Jewish Communities Database, Yizkor Book translations, InfoFiles, Family Tree of the Jewish People, and KehilaLinks, provide critical insights, first-hand accounts, and context about Jewish communal and familial life throughout the world.

Offered as a free resource, JewishGen.org has facilitated thousands of family connections and success stories, and is currently engaged in an intensive expansion effort that will bring many more records, tools, and resources to its collections.

Please visit https://www.jewishgen.org/ to learn more.

Executive Director: Avraham Groll

d

About JewishGen Press

JewishGen Press (formerly the Yizkor Books-in-Print Project) is the publishing division of JewishGen.org, and provides a venue for the publication of non-fiction books pertaining to Jewish genealogy, history, culture, and heritage.

In addition to the Yizkor Book category, publications in the Other Non-Fiction category include Shoah memoirs and research, genealogical research, collections of genealogical and historical materials, biographies, diaries and letters, studies of Jewish experience and cultural life in the past, academic theses, and other books of interest to the Jewish community.

Please visit https://www.jewishgen.org/Yizkor/ybip.html to learn more.

Director of JewishGen Press: Joel Alpert
Managing Editor - Jessica Feinstein
Publications Manager - Susan Rosin

Cover Photo Credits

Cover designed by Rachel Kolokoff Hopper

Front and Back Cover:

Background color and texture: Rachel Kolokoff Hopper

Front and Back Cover Background Photo:
Return to Sender, page vi

Front Cover Photo: Ina and Maurice, memoir cover page

Back Cover Photos:
   Top Left: Ina and Maurice, page 56
   Top Right: Return to Sender, page vi
   Bottom Left: Ina, her sister Felicia, and her two
   brothers, Sevek and Stasiek, page 31
   Bottom Middle: Ina's Parents, page 15
   Bottom Right: Ina's brother Stasiek, his wife Eva, and
their two young sons Aleksander and Michal, page 21

f

And That Was the Last Time
I Saw My Family

A Memoir in Essays
by Ina Teich
(b. 1908, d. 1987)

Edited by her daughter, Judith Teich

For Roni

Contents

Part Three: A New Life in a New Country

Introduction

It was raining hard that morning in March 2019 when my brother and I made the donation of our parents' artifacts to the U.S. Holocaust Memorial Museum. We had carefully wrapped the carton in plastic to protect its precious contents from the unexpected deluge, and I carried the heavy box to the taxi waiting at the curb. After several difficult and upsetting months of combing through these intensely personal materials, I felt a sense of closure. We were placing our family's history into the hands of curators and researchers best qualified to understand and preserve the documents and photos and the story that surrounds them.

Preparing for the donation had prompted my brother and me to finally explore the neglected trove of letters and documents that had been moldering in the back of our closets for years. We unearthed letters in Polish that my parents exchanged when they could not be together: first, during their brief engagement just before the war, when my father was trapped by hostilities in Vienna and my mother was waiting for him in Warsaw. Then, during the war, after they were married and had fled to Cuba, when my mother gained permission to emigrate to the U.S., but my father, under a different immigration quota, was not allowed to join her for over a year. We had not known that they wrote to each other every day during that time.

My brother and I spent hours puzzling over official-looking documents in German and Polish that included, amazingly, even my father's elementary and high school report cards. Some of the yellowed, fragile pages were more than one hundred years old. How had my father managed to save these, when he fled Vienna a few days after his business was confiscated at gunpoint by the Nazis, just a few days before he married my mother in Warsaw? As we sorted through the contents of the boxes, we found many envelopes stuffed with mysterious photos from before the war: relatives and friends, at the beach or picnicking, playing tennis, skiing, laughing. There was no one to ask about these pictures, no one left to tell us who each of these people had been.

Among the papers was an exchange of postcards between my mother, Sabina (she later shortened her name to Ina), and her mother, Justine Szuldiner, from 1940 and 1941. At that time, my mother was living by herself in a boardinghouse in Brooklyn, and my father, Maurice, was still in Cuba, waiting for a visa to the U.S. My mother's parents and siblings had remained behind in Warsaw; by 1941, their neighborhood had become part of the Warsaw Ghetto. In tiny, precise script, the messages on the postcards from Poland avoided any talk of their living conditions, but expressed concern about other family members whose whereabouts were unknown. The last postcard was addressed by my mother in New York to her mother in Warsaw. It was dated September 9, 1941. Stamped across the front, in red ink, were the stark and terrible words, "***Service Suspended—Return to Sender.***"

My interest in our family history had begun decades earlier, when I was eighteen, and my father had prevailed upon me to help him create a draft of his family tree. My older brother had just graduated from college and was preparing for his first trip abroad that summer, and my father was eager for him to meet and reconnect with the shards of our family, the few distant relatives who remained in Europe following the Holocaust. As the first member of our family to visit that continent since my parents fled on the eve of World War II, my brother sort of an emissary.

My father had already made several unsuccessful attempts at designing the tree, using his battered Smith-Corona. Frustrated, he asked me to draw it instead, because my handwriting was smaller and more precise than his, my hand steadier. Neither of us had any idea what a family tree should look like. As the chart took shape, I realized it was riddled with many branches that ended abruptly in 1941 and 1942, with question marks signifying unknown dates and circumstances of deaths. I began to wonder what it might have been like to have known all these people, to have grown up in the midst of this once-large family, surrounded by grandparents, aunts and uncles and cousins.

Twenty-three years later, shortly before her death in 1987, my mother wrote a series of brief, evocative personal essays, which are collected here. They provide colorful detail about her life before the war, her family, their apartment in Warsaw, their joyful summer vacations in the Polish countryside. She wrote about how she was introduced to my father, a sophisticated young bachelor from Vienna, on a blind date. She described their brief courtship and marriage; their wrenching decision to part from their families and the life they knew, and to flee Europe on their own; their voyage to Cuba, the only country that would take them in; and their eventual arrival in the U.S.

The research that my brother and I did over the years, our various attempts to explore and organize our parents' effects, also served to emphasize just how much we don't know—and will probably never know--about our relatives who perished in the Holocaust. I find myself yearning for the missing people--the gatherings, the support, the relationships--that my brother and I, and our children, never had a chance to experience. I can only imagine how much their presence might have enriched our lives.

Echoes of the Holocaust have shaped my life in ways that I cannot grasp and will probably never understand, and the memory of those who did not survive hovers just beyond the borders of my daily life. The more facts we uncover, the more details we learn, the more keenly I feel the enormity of all that was lost.

Note

The essays presented here were written by my mother, Ina Teich, for a class that she took in 1984-85 at the Jewish Community Center in Rockville, MD, where she lived at the time. The class, which was called "My Story," was taught by an English professor from the University of Maryland, and was intended for older people to preserve and share their life experiences. My brother and I had never seen anything similar that my mother had written, and were amazed at how well she expressed herself, particularly since she did not learn English until she was in her 30s. We were extremely happy that we were able to preserve these personal impressions and details of her history.

She died of cancer in November 1987.

Judith Teich
March 2024

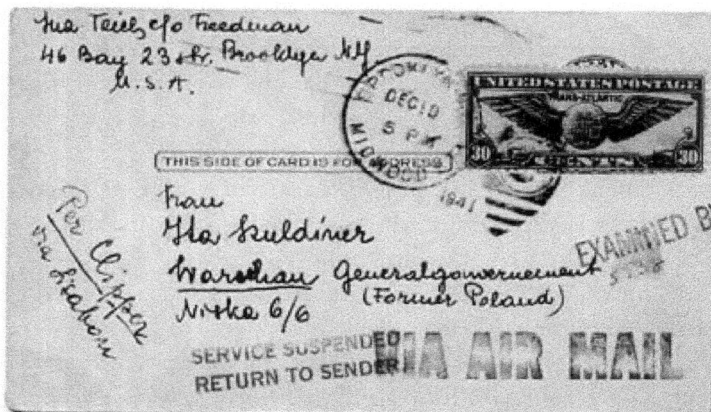

Part One

Life in Warsaw Before the War

And That Was the Last Time I Saw My Family

My Own Dog

Ever since I was a little girl I remember wanting and dreaming about having a dog of my own. Of course, my mother, true to the tradition of most Jewish mothers, did want to have any animal in an apartment where six members of the family and a maid lived, and she strenuously objected to my ideas.

When I look back on my later life when I was married and my own little girl wanted a dog, I know now that I was very unfair to her, for she never had one, because of my objections.

But coming back to the story of my dog, I was pretty lucky. I never gave up either the desire to have my own dog or the hope for a miracle. And the miracle did happen. A friend's dog had puppies, all mixed breed—dachshund and fox terrier. The friend did not have the heart to just get rid of the puppies and she tried to give them a home. When I heard about it, I ran all the way to the friend's house and came home with a two-week-old spotted black and white one-pound bundle of almost fox terrier. I immediately named him "Joke," after a story I had read about a dog of that name, although at the time I did not even know what the word meant.

At first, I had a real hard time with my puppy. Joke was much too young to be weaned from his mother, and for several nights I had to hold him in my arms in my bed to keep him from wandering around and whimpering all night in search of his mother. But I was allowed to keep him and train him myself with a lot of help from our maid who was a country girl who loved animals and knew more about them than any one of us city people. Training was very hard work but also a lot of fun, and I was proud to be the only person whose orders Joke really obeyed.

Joke grew up to be a handsome half-breed fox terrier with very bright, intelligent eyes that did not miss anything. He became a favorite with my whole family, and even my mother grew fond of him. He had his own ways to let me know about his needs and desires. When he was thirsty and his water bowl was empty, he kept banging the bowl all over the kitchen floor. If I pretended that I still did not know what he wanted, he would put his paws on the edge of the kitchen sink and point with his shiny black nose to the faucet.

He knew by some special dog-clock what time I would be coming home from school. He would race from window to window to catch a sight of me on the street and then race to the front door to wait impatiently for my arrival. I was practically knocked down every time by his jumping all over me and licking my face just to show how much he had missed me.

There were times, however, when his exuberance got him and me in trouble. Once, coming back from an outing while the streets were muddy after a rain, he ran away from me and jumped on my mother's bed and trampled all over the freshly laundered bedspread. What happened afterward ended nearly in disaster—only my pleas and tears saved Joke from exile.

The thing he disliked—I can even say hated—most was a bath. As soon as he heard the water running in the bathtub he immediately sought any hiding place he could find, and many times he had to be practically pried from under the bed with a broomstick. I used to be angry with him many times and he knew it. I tried to ignore his attempts to be forgiven. But one look at his sad eyes and hanging tail and he was my love again.

I have a picture of him among my other treasures and I will never forget him. He died of old age at 12 years while I was away on a trip. I was heartbroken when he was not there to greet me when I came home.

Good-bye, Joke. You were a source of a lot of fun and pride for me and I will aways keep my memories of you alive.

After years of pleading with her mother, Ina finally got a puppy when she was 15. "Joke" was an exuberant dachshund-fox terrier mix who loved to play and hated baths. She loved him dearly, and was heartbroken when he died at the age of 12 while she was away on an extended vacation.

Our Apartment

I was born in Warsaw, Poland, the youngest of four children. I do not know how far my memory reaches and how old I was when I first started seeing and understanding things around me. But I had a lot of curiosity and desire to learn.

We lived in a predominantly Jewish part of the town and I really did not have much of an idea of how much antisemitism existed in Poland until I started school. My father owned a wholesale store of all kinds of yarn, which was located on Nalewki Street, the heart of the Jewish business world. My father's customers—apart from large manufacturers—were peasants from surrounding villages. I remember the customary bargaining and the distrust they showed of a Jewish merchant who, according to their thoughts, was only there to cheat them. Many a time they came and left to check other stores not once, but five or six times, until finally coming back with a sheepish smile on their faces and saying, "Your yarn is the nicest and whitest, and the price is not bad."

Our apartment was not very big. It was located on the second floor of a three-story building and contained four or five rooms. Three of the rooms were made into bedrooms; the largest was our parents' bedroom. I remember the furniture, imported from Austria or Germany, which I always considered as the peak of luxury. Made of blond wood with some decorations, the double bed stood on a platform and the beautiful, embroidered bedspread was always carefully arranged. The massive wardrobe was very impressive—the apartments did not have built-in closets—and the white, luxurious curtains on the window held a real magic for a child.

The other rooms were made into children's bedrooms. I shared one with my older sister and the boys had the other bedroom. Strangely, I have no recollections of how these bedrooms were furnished. I imagine they held only plain beds and small wardrobes for clothes.

But I remember well the combined living and dining room, mostly because of a large heating stove that occupied one whole corner of the room. The stove was made of beautiful, light green ceramic tiles, with a multitude of nooks and shelves full of interesting knick-knacks and photographs. It never ceased to enchant me.

I had a special relationship with the beautiful stove. I often stood in front of it, passing my hands over the smooth, shiny tiles. Those stoves were built quite cleverly with many channels that retained heat for a few days once the fire of wood and coal was started. This was just short of a miracle for me at that time.

There was a heavy oak-wood dining table, which could seat twelve or fourteen people. The table had heavy sculptured legs and the whole dining set was my mother's pride and joy. There is a story connected with this table and its beautiful legs. My beloved dog Joke had a habit of hiding under the table. We did not pay any attention to his constant visits under the table. But one day, I heard some strange noises and took a look at Joke sitting comfortably—and what I saw was just short of a disaster! Joke was sharpening his teeth on one of the table legs and had chewed it almost to the breaking point.

You cannot imagine my mother's anger. Joke's fate was hanging by a thread. He must have understood or felt the anger around him and the crime he had committed, because he hid under my bed and no amount of coaxing or threat could get him out of there.

The bathroom was not very elegant but quite large and comfortable. The large bathtub stood on four little legs (chicken legs, I think), and there was cold water. However, for hot water it was necessary to make a fire under a large water tank that stood in the corner of the bathroom. Because of the trouble it took to obtain hot water, a bath was rather a luxury than an everyday habit. One feature was very convenient: there was always a separate unit for the toilet.

The kitchen was big and light. It had a separate entrance for deliveries. I imagine the kitchen was quite primitive, with a plain wood floor, but I did not think of it as primitive at the time. There was a large stove heated by wood and coal; the ashes had to be cleaned out every day. The fire had to be started early, because even breakfast depended on this stove.

The kitchen may have been primitive, but the meals and cakes my mother prepared there were just delicious. Her specialty was a cheese cake that made her famous in our whole large family. I still remember the taste of this cake and none of the cakes I have eaten since have matched this particular taste. Quite a while later, my father acquired a novelty: a two-burner gas range, and this, of course, made the chores in the house a little easier.

There was a small niche off the kitchen, room enough for a bed and a tiny wardrobe. This was a house of our sleep-in maids, and I spent quite a lot of time with young and older maids learning a lot about life from them.

But most of the maids did not stay too long in our service and some did not show up at all. My mother had a reputation of being a very demanding, criticizing employer and the source of information was the janitor of the building. The woman who stayed the longest in our house was Wladislawa Sahogluhowich (what a name!). She was part of our household until I was a teenager, when she died of cancer. I was very sad and I never forgot her and the interesting things she told me about life in her faraway village.

My Parents

Our family was very large. There were many aunts
and uncles on both sides of the family and, of course, a lot
of cousins of all ages whose names I hardly recall now. I
took my family for granted. Everybody I knew had a large
family and I did not appreciate it. When I became a
teenager, I was bored with frequent family gatherings and
often refused to attend them. I know better now. I realize
what a comfort it is to have the support of a large family in
spite of the quarrels, disagreements, and intrigues.

I am sorry that my children never had the privilege
of knowing their grandparents and experiencing their love.
I was the youngest in my family. My sister Felicia was the
oldest; my brother Stasiek was next in age; and my brother
Sevek was closest to my age. Sevek and I spent a lot of
time together and I have a lot of stories to tell about him.
But here I want to write about my mother and father so
that my children will have at least a little glimpse of their
grandparents.

It has been many, many years since, crying, I kissed
my parents goodbye at a crowded railway station on that
never-to-be-forgotten day in November 1938. My husband
and I were leaving Poland, never to come back again and
never to see my parents again. But all I have to do now is
to close my eyes and think of my dad and mom and a
memory of them comes to mind as vivid and alive as if all
those years did not pass at all.

My mother was a handsome woman; she had
beautiful, serious, very dark eyes. Her prematurely gray hair
made a pleasant contrast with her young face. She was an
excellent housekeeper, to the point of being fussy, and she
expected the same perfection from everybody. This was

always a cause of rebellion and resentment among my sister, brothers, and I, but we did learn to be neat. My mother was devoted to her husband, her children, and her home, and I think she was happy in her role as wife, mother, and housewife. There was nothing more expected from a woman in my mother's times. She did not have to look for a career, nor did she have to "prove herself" in any other way.

But my father—how different he was! He had gray eyes with a twinkle, as if he were always thinking of something funny and pleasant. He used to tell us how he had to start working at the age of fourteen to help support his family and he had not had the chance to get a formal education. But he was ambitious and determined to accomplish more in life than merely earning a living. He was an avid reader and he possessed a wonderful ability to learn and absorb a great deal of knowledge. With no help at all, he taught himself to read, write, and speak German, and traveled extensively in Russia and Europe. By the time I was born, he owned a wholesale yarn business and had dealings with important people in the business world.

He became a prominent member of the Jewish community in Warsaw and he served as president of the Jewish Businessmen's Association for many years. He was very helpful to people and in many cases his advice would save people's businesses or solve family problems. I was always very proud when people told me about his "good deeds."

His favorite entertainment was the opera and he could listen for hours to the records on our gramophone, to Caruso and other famous singers. Busy as he was, however, he did not neglect his family. He delighted in taking all four of us children to the circus when it was in town, or to magic shows, or movies, or the theater. We learned about animals from our visits to the menagerie, where animals were kept in cages. (Zoos as they exist now were unknown in my childhood.) He used to take us for rides in the horse-drawn carriages which served as taxis in those days.

But the most fun was in winter when the snow would fall and stay on the ground until spring. As soon as snow covered the streets, instead of carriages, sleighs were hitched to horses wearing jingle-bells. What a delight it was to sit on my father's lap covered with a blanket to keep warm, sliding noiselessly through quiet, snow-covered streets, listening to the sounds of bells and looking at the stars in the sky. Mother seldom joined us in those escapades, but she was always ready to listen to our stories about our adventures. It was so long ago, but I still relive the feeling of security in my parents' love.

My parents are gone now, of course. For many years I did not have any news about them and wondered about their fate. When the news about the horrors of the Holocaust and concentration camps finally began to appear in American newspapers, I was living and working in New York with my husband, after a long separation, and expecting my first child. I was quite happy, but after reading the news, a strange and disturbing feeling of guilt came over me. I could not understand why I was the only member of my family spared from the horror of war, concentration camps, and death. Why indeed?

I do not feel that way now. Some members of my family survived the war. My sister Felicia spent five years in Siberia with her young son before she could go back to the civilized world. My brother Stasiek went through many troubles and dangers. He lost his wife and two sons, but he finally managed to get to Palestine and spent the rest of his life in Israel. My brother Sev was killed by the Nazis. I want my children to know something about him, and I will write about him someday soon.

Although it is not mentioned in her essay, apparently Ina's father was one of the leaders of a boycott of German goods in the late 1930s; he was shot by the Nazis shortly after Warsaw surrendered to the German invasion on September 28, 1939. Her mother died later, either in the Warsaw ghetto or in a concentration camp.

And That Was the Last Time I Saw My Family

My Brother Sevek

Lately I have been thinking about my brother Sevek quite a lot. As children we were constant companions and the memories of the times we spent together come crowding into my mind. I want so much to write about him, and yet every time I start to write, I have to stop. It is almost too painful to write about our happy times when his fate was so cruel.

Recently I submitted the names of my parents and my brother Sevek to Yad Vashem in Jerusalem to be inscribed for posterity as martyrs of the Holocaust. I mourn my parents, of course. But when I think of my brother, a great sadness overcomes me. There were four children in my family. My sister Felicia and my brother Stasiek survived the war and after many adversities managed to pick up the pieces of their ruined lives and return to an almost normal existence.

My sister lost her husband and was exiled by the Russians to a labor camp in Siberia where she spent several years with her small son in very primitive conditions. At the end of the war, she was returned to Poland. She managed to emigrate to France, where she remarried and finally she came to the United States. She still lives in New York.

My brother Stasiek lost his wife and two sons to the Holocaust. After many adventures and experiences in the Polish Army-in-Exile, he managed to get to Israel, where he spent the rest of his life with his second wife.

As for me, of course, I was the luckiest of us all, for I left Europe before the war. There was a lot of trouble and grief in my life, but I was spared the horror of war and

Nazi concentration camps. Even now I ask myself why I was the only one to be spared these experiences.

But my brother Sevek was not lucky at all. Shortly after he was married and started his new life, he and his wife, Mina, were caught in the middle of the nightmare of the Nazi invasion and the Warsaw ghetto. In spite of repeated inquiries we could not find out anything about them, and their fate is unknown. We can only imagine that what happened to other Jews in Poland happened to them. They were so young and never had a chance...

My brother's name was Severyn, but everybody knew him by his nickname, Sevek. He had black, wavy hair and my mother's very dark beautiful eyes. But just as my mother's eyes were calm and serious, his were sparkling and full of mischief. He was only two years older than me, and as children we spent most of the time together, sometimes playing and enjoying each other's company, other times fighting and running to my mother with complaints about each other. Most of the time my mother ignored our quarrels, as she knew quite well that we always made up in the end.

Sevek was curious and inquisitive. He always wanted to know how things were made and how they worked. All my dolls with moveable eyes fell victim to his curiosity. They all ended up with broken heads (which were made of porcelain when I was a little girl.) He just had to find out how the eyes opened and closed. He was always sorry afterwards, when I was in tears over the loss of my doll, but it did not keep him from his next mischief.

He used to hide my books, my toys, even my clothes, and had a grand time watching me look frantically and anxiously for my possessions. This mischievous trait must run in the family. My own son was also teasing his little sister and hiding her things. One time he put her pajamas in—of all places—the freezer, and was having a wonderful time as we were looking for them all over the house. This particular incident brought back to my mind all my childhood memories of the tricks my brother played on me.

My dog, Joke, fell victim many times to Seve's idea of fun. He used to put a hat, eyeglasses, and a necktie on Joke and tried to take him outside to the street in this attire. But my smart Joke always fooled Sevek. He used to hide under a bed and no amount of coaxing would get him out.

Not all of my brother's antics were quite so innocent. Sometimes when I look in the mirror, I can see a tiny scar on the side of my forehead. I close my eyes and see myself as a small, skinny, five-year-old girl and the scene of how the scar happened comes clearly to my mind. Sevek was older, bigger, and stronger than I was, and I always obeyed his commands. This time he ordered me to step on a chair standing by the wall and take down a picture that was hanging over it. What happened next almost ended in disaster—or at least a serious injury. As I climbed on the chair, it collapsed under me and I fell against the wall, hitting my head on the nail from which the picture had hung, narrowly missing my left eye.

The chair had a broken leg. Sevek, following his idea of fun, had arranged the chair so it looked normal. But he surely did not expect his trick to turn out this way. The commotion, yelling, and screaming that followed are hard to describe. Instantly, I was covered with blood and everybody rushed to my rescue. Luckily, the wound was not too serious or deep and healed quite quickly. But it left a scar for life.

Sevek stood in the corner in tears, scared, remorseful and very, very sorry. I could not be angry at him for long, and soon after that we were friends again. However, this experience dampened a little his exuberance and enjoyment of his tricks. As far as I remember, he learned his lesson and never again played any dangerous tricks.

As we grew older, we went our separate ways. We had different friends and different interests in life. Sevek still continued to be happy-go-lucky, not caring much for anything more than his pleasures. He was not a good student and this was a source of constant aggravation for my father, who hoped to give all his children a good education and a good background. In the end, however, Sevek pulled himself together and obtained a diploma (in business administration, I think) from the University of Caen, in northern France.

Outwardly he appeared to be indifferent to the family, but I knew better. He cared deeply for all of us— and I had much proof of it—but his reputation would not let him show any deep emotion, so he pretended indifference.

Eventually, our lives again ran close. He fell in love with Mina, his future wife, about the same time I met my husband. Our weddings were only one day apart. We spent a part of our honeymoon together, forgetting all our problems, having a wonderful time and enjoying each other's company. The last time I saw my brother Sevek was at the railroad station when Maurice and I were leaving Warsaw to start our journey to Cuba. Sevek's eyes were not lively and sparkling that day. In fact, they were full of tears. I knew he hated to see me leave. I miss him still.

And That Was the Last Time I Saw My Family

This is a photo of Ina's brother Stasiek. He initially stayed in Poland with his wife, Eva, and their two young sons Aleksander (b. 1934) and Michal (b. 1938). A few months later, Stasiek was deported to the USSR, although his wife and children remained in Warsaw. He eventually made his way to Palestine; his wife and children perished in the Warsaw Ghetto.

In 1985, Ina prepared a Page of Testimony that she submitted to the archives of Yad Vashem, the Holocaust Museum in Israel. Such "pages" are generally accompanied by a photo; Ina was distraught because she could not find a picture of Sevek. His exact fate and that of his family remains unknown.

And That Was the Last Time I Saw My Family

When I Was Growing Up

The day started early in our household. While most of our family (except me) was still asleep, the maid had to start the fire in the stove so that breakfast could be prepared. A knock at the back door announced the arrival of the milkman. He was an old, skinny little man, bent under the weight of a large metal cannister of raw milk. He poured the milk into a pan specifically prepared for boiling it.

The little man usually left with a smile and a kind good-bye. I liked him and always felt a little sorry for him for working so hard. My mother, however, was always suspicious of him and used to say that the milk tasted watery and she was sure that the little man was adding water to the milk. I, however, could not care less if the milk was watery or not, I liked the little man.

The milk was, of course, boiled to make it safe to drink. When it cooled after boiling, all the cream came to the surface. This cream was my father's favorite addition to his morning cup of coffee and, as nobody else in the family cared even to look at this "delicacy," he had it all to himself.

Another knock at the kitchen door. This time it is the owner of a tiny grocery store from down the street who brought every morning small Kaiser rolls still warm from the oven. They were delicious. I still remember the taste of those rolls spread with real butter.

After breakfast, all the family dispersed. My father went to his store, my brothers and sisters went to school and, as I was too young to go to school, I was left home with the maid. My mother was helping my father in the store and in a little while she also left after giving a thousand instructions to the maid.

So there I was with nothing to do, and I imagine I was constantly in the maid's way while she was trying to do her chores and start the midday dinner. The family gathered at the dinner, which my mother came home early to cook. Everybody thought she was a very good cook, but I would be a very bad judge because I really was not at all interested in food.

I was small and skinny, and a very finicky eater which was a constant worry to my mother. She used to take me to different doctors who always pronounced me in very good health and assured my mother that even if I did not eat much, I would not die of starvation. But my mother would not give up. After so many years, I still have the picture in my mind of my mother running after me around the table with a bowl of soup and a spoon, and trying to encourage me to eat. She was seldom successful—the more she insisted, the less I ate.

I do not really remember any special dishes my mother prepared, but always our holiday dinner was big and festive. The menu: chopped liver, gefilte fish, or otherwise chicken soup with noodles, boiled chicken and boiled beef. For dessert there was fresh fruit compote and parve cake. (Sound familiar?) This is all I can recall. I suppose there were some variations in the menu, but I really do not remember.

Some of this tradition was observed in my own house. But there was one item that I never tried to imitate. Every Saturday we had "cholent." It was prepared on Friday: meat, barley, and potatoes cut in quarters were put in a special pot, covered with brown paper with our name on it, and sent to the baker for a 24 hour slow cooking. It was brought home again on Saturday afternoon, still hot from the oven and this is one meal I remember enjoying. Especially the potatoes were all brown and full of flavor. Well, enough about food and let's continue the story of our life at that time.

Once a month we had a special cleaning woman for a most thorough cleaning. The house for a while looked like a disaster area. The furniture was pulled back from the walls and every bit of dust was cleaned away. All the rugs (I do not remember how many there were) were picked up from the floor, taken outside, and put on a special stand just for this purpose, and beaten with a tool (I do not remember the English name for it) resembling a tennis racquet (without the holes) until not a speck of dust was left. The walls were all wallpapered and there must have been some pictures, but I have no recollection of any of them. It was a lot of work to put everything back in place, but after this cleaning the house smelled new and fresh. We all were very careful not to spill anything, not wanting to provoke my mother's anger and reproaches.

Also about once a month these was a day of "big" laundry. Most of our dresses and underwear were washed by hand and ironed, but the sheets, pillow cases and towels, etc., had to have a special laundress to perform at least two days of washing on a washboard, boiling and mangling.

A big, big wooden basin was taken out of the basement and big pails of water were continually boiling on the stove. I was not allowed in the kitchen because of the danger of so much hot water.

While the cleaning and laundering was going on, I usually sought my hideaway. We had two balconies and on one of them, with the help of one of our peasant maids, I created a little garden. Our janitor secured wooden boxes to the railing. I took good care of my garden. I had pretty little flowers, sweet peas, and, my pride and joy, honest-to-goodness large sunflowers growing in a big bucket of dirt. They were complete with seeds that everybody tasted.

The balcony was my window to the world of nature. There was nothing of outdoors in our narrow, cobblestone street, with no trees or grass anywhere. Few people thought of any kind of plants in their houses, but I have loved plants all my life. When the time came to go to the country on summer vacation, I was overjoyed. To be surrounded by trees, grass and flowers—it was a real treat!

Summer in the Country

Every summer, as far back as I remember, as soon as school was over, my family would go to the country. For me, the youngest of four children, not yet old enough to attend school, going to the country was an event of great importance. I always started my preparations early, endlessly discussing with my mother and my sister which clothes to take, which toys and books. Even the preparation and anticipation were a source of great excitement to me.

Finally, a horse-drawn wagon would stop in front of our apartment building and I remember running up and down the stairs (we lived on the third floor) announcing to anybody who would listen that we really were going to the country.

Of course, we children had to help load the wagon with all the household articles, bedding, linen, clothes, and toys. The wagon would take most of the day to arrive at our cottage, though the small village where it was located was close to Warsaw (Poland) were my family and I lived.

We—my mother, my sister, my brothers and the maid—would ride the train. The trip, I know now, was no longer than one to one and a half hours, but to a small child it seemed like an expedition into the unknown. The wagon with our belongings was already waiting in front of the cottage, and among shouts of joy and excitement and a lot of confusion, all of our belongings were unloaded and summer in the country would become a reality.

Our rented cottage was one of a colony of identical cottages, rustic and quite primitive, each equipped with a veranda where most of our meals were served. The place was practically swarming with children of all sizes and ages who were running, screaming, and laughing. Dogs, cats and chickens were also running loose, and the confusion that resulted was hard to describe.

Soon we all got to know each other, to like some of the kids, and to hate and fear the big bullies. We all played together most of the time, though we also quarreled, fought fiercely, and complained. But in the end, we parted friends for life—or so we thought.

Our maid, who was a country girl, occasionally took us, with my mother's permission, to the nearby woods to pick berries and mushrooms. My mother trusted our maid, who was with us from the time I was a baby, and she knew that Wladyslawa was an authority on edible berries and mushrooms. What great fun it was to go with her! We used to scatter around to look for berries and mushrooms, showing here every handful for approval. We were happy with the freedom to run to our heart's desire, and sang anything that came to our minds at the top of our voices, laughing all the time at nothing.

One summer Wladyslawa gave me a little chick for my birthday. Together we raised it as a pet. I called it Chip-Chip. It became so tame that it followed me around and ate from my hand. But shortly Chip-Chip grew to become a chicken with snowy white feathers and yellow legs and was ready to lay eggs. I will never forget the sight of my chicken, doing a little dance and proudly shaking her tail. It was her way of announcing a great accomplishment— laying her first egg.

My father did not stay with us during the weekdays. We all missed him, especially me. Everybody was saying that I looked just like my father, and I was very proud of that. My father always came each Friday afternoon to spend the weekend with us.

I loved my father not only because he was my father, but because he was a smart and jovial man, full of jokes and funny stories, and I always waited impatiently for his arrival. The tracks of the train he was riding ran just outside our cottage colony. We always waited by the fence for my father to throw his bag through the [train] car window as was his habit. We raced to retrieve the bag, knowing that there always would be a surprise for us in it. Oh, it was a lot of fun to spend summer in the country.

But one particular summer is etched more sharply in my memory than all the other summers. That year was not long after the "war to end all wars" (World War I) ended; the war was still very much on the minds of grown-ups. They talked and discussed endlessly the people who were killed, wounded, and missing. The effect of this atmosphere of gloom on the children was really quite profound.

All that summer we played a game of war. We formed two camps and seriously considered the other camp as an "enemy camp." We dug trenches and stayed in them for hours, calling names and exchanging insults with the enemy camp. The boys dressed as soldiers and generals and collected all the toy guns they could find. The girls were nurses, of course, with white caps and armbands with Red Crosses on them. Unfortunately, we carried the "enemy" idea beyond the game. We actually disliked our "enemies" for no more reason than the stirred-up feelings. As in real life, the war, battles, and quarrels did not solve anything at all.

The summers stopped when I reached school age. My older sister and brothers thought of different ideas for vacations. The memories of the carefree days linger in my mind. I had a very happy childhood, full of love and attention. We tried—my husband and myself—to give our children happy memories about carefree childhood days. I hope that we succeeded.

This is the earliest picture of Ina. She seems to be around two years old in this staged studio photo. Her older sister Felicia, appears to her left and her two brothers, Sevek and Stasiek are on the right.

And That Was the Last Time I Saw My Family

Prayer in the Classroom

When I read about the controversy about prayer in the classroom, the half-forgotten memories of my own years as a Jewish girl in a predominantly Catholic school come vividly to mind. Feelings and experiences which I have not thought about for many years come back to me, and I see myself as a small girl in a classroom of forty children with only two other Jewish girls.

I do not know why my parents enrolled me in this private Catholic school when quite a few Jewish schools for girls were available in Warsaw. What puzzles me still more is that my older sister went to a Jewish school, and so did my two brothers. I should have asked them when I could, but now there is nobody to ask. But...here I was and very much excited about going to school. I was looking forward to wearing a uniform, which consisted of a pleated purple skirt, a white blouse and a black beret with a purple bow. I felt important, and anticipated a lot of fun.

The school was not a religious school in the full sense of the word. It was not connected to any church in particular, and almost all of the teachers were lay teachers; they were not even all Catholics, but, of course, there was not a single Jewish teacher. There was no separation of church and state in Poland, and religion was evident everywhere. The school principal was a tall, slender distinguished-looking "old maid" with a constant saccharin smile on her face, very rigid and devout. The rumors circulating about her told of a tragic love affair in her youth that made her what she was: strict and unyielding.

There was, of course, a priest on the staff who took care of all the religious matters and taught religion to the Catholic children. He was a kind enough man, but when he tried to talk to the Jewish girls he used to say things which were foreign to us and we tried to avoid him, because we were a little afraid of him and his talk.

My first day of school was very painful. As we assembled in the classroom in the morning, the first thing the home room teacher told everybody was to kneel down and recite the morning prayer. I knew that the prayer was a Christian prayer, and I remained standing. The teacher was very annoyed and sharply repeated the command to kneel down.

I was scared, but I had no choice—I gathered all my courage and said loudly, "I am Jewish and I am not allowed to take part in Christian prayers!" This time the teacher let me and the other Jewish girls stand up during the prayer, but from then on, I became a target for a lot of comments and harassment from her and later from some of my classmates.

I was reprimanded time and time again for not showing enough respect for religion, and no matter what I did, the teacher always found fault with my behavior during the prayer. I never said anything to my family about all that was going on in school. I was a good little girl and did not want to worry them.

I fared much better with the other teachers. I learned quickly and enjoyed studying. My favorite subject was languages. I was good in French, wrote good essays in Polish, but strangely enough, Latin intrigued me the most. In fact, I became the teacher's favorite student. I remember one particular time, for reasons I do not recall, that I came to class completely unprepared and praying that I would become invisible. But…the teacher called on me to read and translate the paragraph assigned to the class. I got really scared and timidly admitted that I had not even looked at this paragraph. "Read it anyway," was the teacher's reply. I had no choice—with a shaky voice, I started to read this paragraph, and I was amazed that I understood every word. I did the translation correctly, but I was still expecting to be punished for not doing my homework. Instead, I received a high mark with the comment 'Ex promptu' (unprepared).

The daily prayers and kneeling in class and unpleasantness of being singled out stopped bothering me after a while, and I did my best to ignore the hostile glances of the teacher and some of the girls. I had been quite unprepared for this situation. Until I went to school, I never experienced the sting of antisemitism which, of course, was ever present in Poland. My family lived in a Jewish section of the city and until my school years I had little contact with the gentile world.

At first things in school were not too bad; I even managed to become friends with some girls. But as the years went by, the atmosphere in school changed completely. Prompted by the course that the Polish government was taking, some older, mean-minded girls became leaders of action against the Jewish girls. Some of my friends among the rest of the class tried to keep contact with me, but they in turn were harassed and bothered, so they finally gave up. Now we, the three Jewish girls, were isolated and alone. There were nasty comments, name-calling, and I remember receiving nasty anonymous telephone calls at home. I have no idea whether the principal or the teachers were aware of the extent of what was going on; we were too proud to report it. All I know is that no one tried to stop it.

The atmosphere was tense and unhealthy and full of resentment. Even when things were calmer, I did not trust the friendship of any of the gentile girls. I could not wait for graduation and was very happy when my days at that school were over. All of my experiences there had made me distrustful of the Polish people.

We Jewish girls were pushed into kind of a "ghetto," but in spite of the isolation, we managed to enjoy life. We became very friendly and I developed a long and close friendship with one of the girls, Halina Kobryner. Our friendship survived her marriage and mine, up to my departure from Poland. We exchanged letters for a while, but we completely lost contact when the war broke out. I never heard from her or about her again.

While I was in school, I started to dream about someplace in the world where a Jew could live and be proud of being a Jew. I wished not to hear any more in my life the call, "Dirty Jew!" or "Jew, go to Palestine!" But that was exactly the place where I wanted to go. I started to make plans that some day I would go there and experience the feeling of being among my brothers and sisters.

I had to wait several years for my wish to come true, but I did go to visit Palestine…but that, again, is another story.

Ina is seated second from the right in the fifth row (a red dot above her head identifies her).

And That Was the Last Time I Saw My Family

The Land of My Dreams: Part I

I attended a Catholic school in Warsaw, Poland, where I was born and where I grew up. In school, I was constantly exposed to the hostile attitudes of my Gentile schoolmates who made my life miserable. These experiences proved to have a very profound effect on me. I kept wishing and dreaming about finding myself in a place where a Jew would not have to constantly defend his Jewishness in the face of sneers and name-calling, a place where to be a Jew might be a source of pride and pleasure and not a curse. I knew about only one such place— Palestine.

Palestine was my dream and I kept wishing I could go there and experience, if only temporarily, the feeling of being myself, the feeling of real freedom. My dream was shared by many young Jewish people from Poland, Russia, Lithuania, and Latvia, who were willing to leave a comfortable life behind and help build a Jewish homeland. This, of course, was the dream of Theodore Herzl, the founder of modern Zionism. Most of these young Jewish people were idealists who wanted to take part in creating a new life for Jews from all over the world in Palestine.

Palestine was a British mandate at the time, and the British did not make it easy for the Jews to enter the mandate. But in spite of all the problems and restrictions, the young Zionists were flocking to the "promised land." Among these young people were good friends of mine, Lena and Bolek Blechstein. They were newly married, and instead of settling in Warsaw, as their parents had urged them to do, they decided to emigrate to Palestine. They knew only too well about my feelings and my dreams, and they invited me to come and stay with them for a while, as soon as they got settled. I could not believe my good fortune! My dream was going to be fulfilled!

Travel to the Middle East in the late 1930s was not as easy and uncomplicated as a trip to Israel is now. All you need now is a passport and the money for an airplane ticket. It takes only ten or eleven hours to reach Israeli soil from the East Coast of the United States. Coming to Israel today, you might experience a sense of great pride and admiration for the Israeli accomplishments, as well as enjoying the sightseeing. But for me it was different. My feelings and impressions after years of longing and a long journey were deeper, more exciting, and never to be forgotten.

I started planning my journey almost immediately. I could not think or talk about anything else, and I am sure that I bored a lot of people with my constant talk about Palestine. But I did not care. Of course I needed a lot of help in making arrangements, and also a lot of financial help. My father always stood by me when I needed any advice or help.

When I look back at this time of my life, I see things that I did not see then. My father was so helpful, so eager, and just as excited as I was in discussing the details of my trip with me, and I realize now that he was fulfilling his own wish. There were so many things to take care of— passport, Romanian and British visas, and (because of British immigration policy), money to deposit at the British consulate to assure my return. My father was of great help, and I did not have to worry about the financial part of my adventure.

My voyage was quite complicated, long and tiring, but also very interesting and romantic. I boarded a train in Warsaw and was on my own. I was on my way to the

Romanian port of Constanza on the Black Sea. The train ride was long and not too exciting. However, I managed to get acquainted and become friendly with a few young Jewish people who were also going to Palestine. One of them, a young dancer and actor from Riga, Latvia—Sasha was his name—became my constant companion during my entire stay in Palestine. He also had a dream to create a Jewish theater in Palestine. (I do not think he was very successful in his effort.)

When the train arrived in Constanza, it rode straight into the port. There, right before my eyes, was the great ship, so that it seemed all I had to do was to stretch out my arm and touch it. It was so exciting! There was no need for any transportation from the train to the ship. All the passengers simply walked up the gangway.

I do not remember how long we were at sea, but I do remember that I was almost sorry the journey was coming to an end. We all had a wonderful time. We were young and full of life. We expected only good things to happen to us. We flirted, played games, ran, and did exercises. We danced and kept dancing late into the night.

The ship stopped twice on the way to Palestine. We docked in Istanbul, Turkey. We were allowed to go ashore for sightseeing. It was my first look into the Islamic world and I was fascinated by the splendor and wealth of the mosques and the strange customs that forced women to cover their faces.

The second stop we made was at Piraeus, the Greek port on the Aegean Sea. I remember Athens as a city full of beautiful flowers. We took a tour of Athens, visiting all the classical sights, the Acropolis and the temples of all the mythological gods I remembered from my school history books. It was a feeling of looking into the ancient past.

Finally, we arrived in Jaffa. I was at last in Palestine, the land I had dreamed about for so many years. I wondered whether my experiences would live up to my expectations...

Several of Ina's friends from Warsaw, who had emigrated to Palestine, invited her for an extended visit in 1935. On the way she became friendly with several young Jewish people who were also going to Palestine.

Here Ina is walking along a rural road in Israel, possibly in an orange grove on a moshav, a collective farm.

And That Was the Last Time I Saw My Family

The Land of My Dreams: Part II

As I started to write about my visit to Palestine in this second part of "Land of My Dreams," I stopped to think for a moment. So many great changes have taken place in that area and so much has happened that there is hardly anything left of the ideal land I saw through my young eyes. But my memory of the Jewish Palestine the way it was then, and even my own feelings, are still so vivid that I feel it is worth writing about them.

The sight that greeted my eyes when I disembarked from the ship in the port of Jaffa was confusing and not at all what I had expected to see. Instead of young Jewish kibbutzniks, we were surrounded by a crowd of Arabs milling around and constantly shouting things I could not understand. They were dressed in very strange clothes. They wore trousers, tight at the ankles, which formed a sack-like fullness in the back. They also wore head-coverings of striped cloth. This is now a very familiar sights on the head of Yasir Arafat and others (and as I learned later, it is called a "keffiyah"). But for me at the time I arrived in Jaffa, all those things were quite strange and unfamiliar to my inexperienced eyes.

I felt lost, realizing that I was in Arab territory. I looked around anxiously to see my friends who were to meet my ship at Jaffa and I felt a twinge of fear when I could not find them. But just then, I noticed a crowd of people in a cordoned-off space, quite a distance away, shouting and waving their arms. British police were holding this crowd back and not letting anyone come close to the disembarking passengers. My friends were in the crowd, of course, but I had to wait until after all the controls and many, many questions were over before I could greet and embrace my friends. Only then did I get the feeling that I had really arrived in Palestine.

The taxi ride to Tel Aviv was short. I kept looking out the window, but all I could see was sand and dust—no trees, no flowers, and only occasional tin-can huts. This was the Arab territory. The landscape started changing as we got closer to Tel Aviv. There were gardens, blooming shrubs, and neat little houses.

I immediately fell in love with Tel Aviv. I loved the white buildings with balconies, so different from the gray and somber architecture of Warsaw. The sky was incredibly blue, and the sun so bright that everything seemed to be bathed in light.

My friends were helpful and eager to show me around, but they were very busy. Bolek was a bus driver for a cooperative called Hamaavir, and was working long hours. Lena was quite absorbed in her domestic duties. I did not want to interfere with their life style, and I was very happy when my friend from the ship, Sasha, from Riga, Latvia, looked me up and we began to spend a lot of time together. He did not know Polish and I did not speak Russian, but strangely enough we did not have any trouble communicating. We roamed the streets of Tel Aviv, stopping to eat felafel or watermelon from the street vendors.

The first few weeks I was living in a dream world, with my head in the clouds. I looked around and saw the smiling faces of young people, sturdy, handsome, and suntanned. I kept telling myself—all those people, the bus drivers, policemen, construction workers, shopkeepers—all of them were my brothers and sisters. And it was sheer happiness to walk the streets feeling sure of myself and really free.

In my eyes, Jewish Palestine was a country as close to ideal democratic society as one could imagine. In contrast to my experiences in Poland, there was practically no crime, no robberies, and of course no killing. The doors of the houses and apartments were left unlocked, without fear of burglary or theft. (All of this is of course forgotten in modern Israel.) I remember one incident when I forgot my purse on the beach and, to my surprise, found it untouched in the same place when I came back later looking for it.

It was also a classless society. The exodus of Jews from Nazi Germany had just started and there were a lot of highly educated people who mingled freely with ordinary laborers and worked together on simple jobs without feeling that the work was below their status.

I toured the country, sometimes with Sasha, more often alone. There were no frontiers, no restrictions, and nobody felt the Arabs were enemies. I visited Jerusalem and the Dead Sea, traveled through the Judean Hills and followed the Jordan River. I loved everything; all those places evoked so many feelings and brought the Bible to life for me.

It was such a pleasure to visit the Kibbutzim and to see the people working in harmony for a common goal—building a Jewish homeland. It was a wonderful time in my life and I know I will never forget it. But, of course, after a few weeks, my euphoria began to wear off a little. I started to see the real life of the people of Palestine with all of their problems, disappointments, and disagreements. However, none of the people I saw, no matter how unhappy, would have exchanged their lives in Palestine for more comfortable lives in the countries in which they had grown up.

The three months of my visa went by all too quickly. I really hated to leave. Sasha wanted me to marry him and stay in Palestine for good. But I was not ready to leave my family. I liked him a lot, and we were very good friends, but I was not in love with him, and my feelings for him were not strong enough. So finally, it was time to end my "dream trip" and return to reality, to my family and my life. I said goodbye to all my friends and the land I had learned to love.

My homecoming was not all joyous. My beloved dog, Joke, did not greet me at the door as was always his way. He had died while I was away, but I did not know about it. He was 12 years old and died of old age. I have never forgotten him.

The second time I went to the Middle East was many years later when I was married and our children were quite grown. Many changes took place in those many years. Israel had become an independent state and had fought several wars. Maurice was Zionist all his life and the visit to Israel was also his cherished dream. I was happy and fascinated watching him and seeing that he experienced the same feelings of "coming home" as I did many years ago.

Maurice died about one and a half years after our visit to Israel. I was very sad for a long time, but every time I remembered the face of my husband when we landed in Israel, I had a good and warm feeling that he, too, had his dream fulfilled, and I was able to witness and share his happiness.

And That Was the Last Time I Saw My Family

Ina had not seen her brother Stasiek, who had emigrated to Palestine after the war, since she left Poland in late 1938. Maurice, who was an ardent Zionist, had long dreamed of visiting Israel, but this was his first trip there. It was in 1966, less than two years before he died. Their expressions clearly convey their happiness.

And That Was the Last Time I Saw My Family

Part Two

Fleeing Europe, Parting from Family

And That Was the Last Time I Saw My Family

Falling in Love

It was December 1937 in Warsaw, Poland. I mention this date because it becomes very important later in my life. The world was still at peace, but the threat of war disaster hung heavily in the air. Things were happening in the world which were to affect all our lives. But I was young and optimistic, not paying much attention to the world news, caring more for my own comfort and pleasure.

One day my good friend Ruth, recently married to a man from Vienna, called me up and asked for a favor. She had a houseguest, her husband's brother, and she needed somebody to entertain him and show him around Warsaw and surroundings. She was too busy, or so she told me, to spare the time. Besides, she felt that he would enjoy the company of some of her unmarried friends. I jumped to the idea. I wasn't dating anybody I particularly liked at that time, and the prospect of meeting a man from the West was extremely appealing to me. People from Western Europe were considered very sophisticated; besides, this would be an occasion to practice what little German I knew at the time.

Ruth did not even bother to introduce us, but arranged a blind date, of all places, on a street corner. It might seem strange nowadays, but at the time of my youth it was quite acceptable and usual to meet people that way. It was also arranged that to avoid any mistakes and to recognize each other, he was supposed to carry a book and I was to carry a patent leather purse and a white handkerchief in my suit pocket.

I was pretty nervous as I approached the street corner, almost regretting that I had agreed to the arrangement. A thought occurred to me; it would be a very uncomfortable situation if we disliked each other. But I was there--I saw a man standing there and it was too late to retreat. He was slender, slightly built and carefully and elegantly dressed. He had the most gentle and handsome face I ever saw. My heart skipped a beat--he was carrying a book!

I never believed in "love at first sight", but we had one look at each other and it happened, we fell in love on the very first date.

We spent days and evenings sightseeing, going to cafes and talking, talking about our lives and our interests which seemed to be very much alike. I did not confide to my family, but everybody noticed a change in me and they knew that something was happening.

Finally, we had to make our love official. I brought him home for Friday dinner. Everybody gathered there, my sister and her husband, my brother and his wife, my brother Sev who gave up his date for the evening to be with the family and meet his sister's love. Maurice--my future husband--gained the hearts of all of the members of my family and the atmosphere at the dinner was pleasant and happy.

I was happier than I ever was in my life and excited about the future in beautiful Vienna. I gave little thought to the feelings of my parents, who hated to see me move so far away. Only later I learned that my mother was crying in secret at the thought that her youngest, her baby was leaving the nest.

Vienna was not really that far away from Warsaw and little did she know that shortly I would be going away much farther and would never see her again.

Maurice had to go back to Vienna after his four-week visit in Warsaw, to attend to his business and prepare for our life together, and I settled down to wait impatiently for his return. We exchanged letters daily and talked about love, life, and the beautiful future. But suddenly a disaster struck--the Nazis took over Vienna and all our plans turned to ashes. I was in despair, all I wished for was for Maurice to be able to get out of Vienna and join me in Warsaw. I did not care about anything else. Nothing else was important. He did manage to get out, we did get married, but our life turned out to be quite different from what we planned. But that is another story.

This photo shows Ina and Maurice at a restaurant, on their first date. It was probably taken by an itinerant photographer, which was not unusual at the time.

The Decision

Our wedding was set for 2 April 1938. The time was short; my mother was very busy with preparations and anxious to get everything ready on time. Just then, my brother Sev suddenly decided to get married at the same time and his decision added to the general confusion. There was talk about a double wedding, but this idea was quickly abandoned because we had different ideas on what kind of wedding we wanted. Mina, my brother's bride, had her heart set on a real fancy ceremony, complete with a long gown, long veil, and a big reception. I felt differently; a big fancy wedding was not suitable under the circumstances under which we found ourselves, Maurice and I. Besides, what I really felt was that I did not want to share this important day with anybody, even my brother. So, a compromise was reached. Our wedding was on Saturday night and Sev and Mina's on Sunday afternoon. Our ceremony was modest--I wore a white tailored suit and a small hat with a veil. The reception was at my parents' house.

Years later, I learned that the synagogue where we were married is the only one left standing, practically undamaged, in Warsaw, while all the other temples were burned and razed to the ground. I don't know exactly why, but this news gave me a good feeling.

After the weddings, we went to the mountains for a short honeymoon. There we met with my brother and his wife. We forgot about all our problems and had a few wonderful days together--two young couples in love and full of joy in being together. But it was time for me and Maurice to go back to Warsaw and face in earnest the reality of our uncertain future. We had continuous discussions with my parents and family. They wanted, of course, for us to stay in Poland. My father offered all the help he could give us in earning a living, if only Maurice listened to "reason" and his suggestions. But all the discussions did not change the reality of the situation. While Poland was still at peace, there were ominous signs that peace was not going to last. My father, like so many other people, was deluding himself, reassuring everybody by saying that "things will quiet down and life will return to normal."

I could not understand and still cannot get over the wonder that my father, smart, intelligent and experienced man that he was, could have been so utterly naive. Maurice had a very different picture of the world in that year of 1938. With uncanny, almost prophetic accuracy, he predicted the war and the fate of the Jews in Europe. And I believed him.

His idea was to leave Europe--the sooner, the better. After weeks of endless discussions, which failed to convince my father or us, we finally announced our decision to emigrate. But where to? We longed to go to Palestine, which was my husband's dream from the time he was a small boy. But for many reasons, it was out of the question. We couldn't afford to wait for visas. The same was true for the South American countries, and to get a U.S. visa meant waiting not months but years because of the immigration quota policy.

Just then we happened to meet a woman who, a few years earlier, had married a man from Cuba and who was in Warsaw visiting her family. She and her husband were doing quite well and she painted the picture of life in Habana in rosy colors. No visa was required, and only a $500 per person deposit was needed on arrival to insure that the immigrants would not become a "burden" on the Cuban society. All this seemed pretty promising, and we decided that Cuba was to be our new home.

We tried to think of our decision as an adventure, but deep inside we were scared, really scared, and had many doubts and misgivings. But we never admitted this to my family. We were acting as if everything was normal-- we went to the movies and the theater, we got together with friends and family. And the time passed.

We had to be prepared, at least in a small way, to make a living in a strange country. My husband succeeded in getting representations from Polish manufacturers, and I took a course in hand sewing luxurious leather gloves. (Needless to say, I never earned a penny with this unique skill.) We hoped all these preparations would help in our life struggle in a strange world.

Finally, the day of our departure arrived. We were to take a train to Gdynia, a Polish port on the Baltic Sea, to board a ship which was to take us to LeHavre, France, on the first lap of our journey to Cuba. All this extra travel was to avoid passing through Nazi Germany, which was, of course, out of the question. I will never forget the sight of all our family and friends gathered at the railroad station shouting goodbyes and good wishes. I was saying goodbye to everybody with a smile and my eyes were dry. Then I noticed that my mother was standing at the back of the crowd as if she were waiting for something. Suddenly, I remembered what she had once told me: according to Jewish tradition, before going away, you reserve your last kiss and embrace for your mother. I ran to her and threw my arms around her and both of us burst out crying.

And that was the last time I saw my family.

Ina and Maurice were married in Warsaw on April 2, 1938; this is their wedding portrait. They left from Gdynia, Poland in November 1938. The first leg of their journey took them to France; they had to go by sea in order to avoid passing through Nazi Germany.

The "bear" apparently was a popular winter mascot of this mountain resort town, Zakopane, Poland, where Ina and Maurice went for a brief honeymoon. The other couple might possibly be Ina's brother Sevek and his wife Mina, who were married the day after Ina and Maurice and joined them for part of their honeymoon.

The Journey

As the train carried us away from Warsaw, away from the security of the family, its help and experience, we finally found ourselves face to face with the full impact of our decision. We sat in silence for a long time, both of us with our private thoughts and fears. We were on our own now, all our decisions and mistakes would be our sole responsibility. What if it would be impossible to earn a living? What would happen to us?

My thoughts were grim, but in spite of doubts and fears, a little excitement began to filter in. After all, we were young, we had a lot of time ahead of us, and we were together. Just then, I felt my husband's arm around me as whispered into my ear, "Don't worry, I promise you we will make it. Even if life may be tough, we have each other." These words became our key words. We had to repeat them often when times were hard and we were close to despair. And somehow it always helped us to hope for a better life. One other little glimmer of hope also sustained us. Thanks to my father's insistence, we had registered for immigration to the United States. We realized that we might have to wait several years for our entry visas, but still it was a possible way to get a second chance if life in Cuba proved impossible for us. As it turned out, this is exactly what happened.

In the morning, we arrived in Gdynia and went directly to the harbor. We had to go through a humiliating search by the emigration officials. I still cannot imagine what the authorities were looking for. We boarded a Polish ship named "Batory" (if my memory serves me correctly). The weather was bad and the sea was very stormy. I became seasick almost immediately and could not leave my berth for two days.

Maurice did not suffer from seasickness and spent most of the time outside on deck, mostly on my insistence. He kept coming down to our cabin every half hour and tried to get me to put on some clothes and come outside with him to get some fresh air. But it was to no avail. I was feeling too miserable to care. Every time Maurice came down to our cabin, he took a sip of cognac from a bottle somebody had brought to the railroad station as a going-away present. The expression on the face of my non-drinking husband, trying to convince me that the only reason he was drinking the liquor was that it kept him from becoming seasick, was just too funny and I couldn't help laughing in spite of my seasickness and discomfort.

At last the weather improved and I joined the other passengers on deck. We made friends with a few young couples who, like ourselves, were looking for a new life away from Europe. The time went by quickly and soon we arrived at Le Havre in the north of France. From there we took a cross—country train to Paris, where my father's younger brother had lived for many years with his wife and young daughter. We had promised to visit them on our way to Cuba and we were looking forward to seeing them as well as the famed city of Paris. My first impression, however, was not too favorable. Our luggage was missing and the first thing we had to do was to shop for a change of clothes. The luggage, fortunately, was found the next day.

I was anticipating a very pleasant visit. I liked my Uncle Joseph and his family. But the mood in Paris was not "gay;" in fact it was quite subdued. Nazi Germany was just too close for comfort and everybody was faced with just as uncertain a future as we were. We did manage to visit the Louvre, various historic sights, and the Eiffel Tower, which somehow did not seem quite as impressive as it been described. My relatives were extremely nice and helpful. We also met several friends of my husband who were lucky enough to have managed to leave Vienna in time.

We soon began to feel restless and impatient, however; it was time to continue our journey. We took a train to the south of France, to the port of La Rochelle Palice, where we were to board a British ship called "Ordunia, which was owned by the Cunard Line and was going to several South American countries besides Cuba.

When we arrived at the harbor, we were met with a scene of utter confusion. The ship was anchored about a mile away from shore and the passengers were being transported to it by small motor boats. The waves were high, the little boats were bobbing dangerously up and down, and people were frightened and screaming. The worst was still to come. To get on the deck, we had to climb rope ladders from the bobbing, unsteady motor boats. The older people were helped by sailors, but even with their help, there were a few near accidents. I think I will never forget this scene: people scrambling all around, parents looking for children, children looking for parents, all the time shouting and crying.

When all the passengers were finally on board and the confusion cleared up, we looked at the European shore fading in the distance and once again sadness came over us. Farewell to my happy childhood and secure youth. I left it all behind. A new era in my life was about to begin.

And That Was the Last Time I Saw My Family

Ina and Maurice sailed first from Gdynia, Poland, to Le Havre, France, then made their way to the port of La Rochelle Palice. There they boarded a ship called the Orduña, which took them to Cuba via Liverpool, England, and Bermuda. Although they were refugees with an uncertain future, they decided to try and treat the voyage as a holiday.

On the Way to Cuba

Travel on the ship Ordunia proved to be entirely different from what I had anticipated. I was afraid that a ship full of refugees would be a very depressing place to be. We would hear a lot of heartbreaking stories, adding to our own sad experiences.

But, surprisingly, it turned out to be just the opposite. Most people wanted to forget, at least for a while, why they found themselves on board this ship, and wanted to enjoy the few weeks at sea before all of us would have to face the reality of a new life in a strange country. We were making believe that we were on vacation, on a sea cruise, treated as guests and well taken care of. We were served three meals a day without a need to shop, cook, or wash dishes. If the food was not always to our taste—British cuisine is not known for excellence—this did not dampen our spirits. The ship carried some South Americans returning home, but mostly there were European refugees bound to different South American countries.

We were friendly with a lot of people, but we became really close with a young couple from Vienna who had managed to get away in time. We had a lot in common with them. Just like us, they were married only recently, and just like us, their high hope for the future turned to ashes.

We spent a lot of time together, talking for hours about ourselves, our lives, disappointments and worries. We regretted that our friendship would be a short one, for we were to part at the end of our journey. We were going to Cuba and they were bound for Bolivia. We promised to keep in touch, but we knew we would never see each other again. For a long time, we exchanged letters describing our impressions and experiences in our new homes, but we never met again. I still have among my treasured mementoes a tiny flower pin given to me by my friend on the ship, whose name, I am sorry to say, I cannot recall.

Most of the time the weather was beautiful, the sea quiet and peaceful. No land was to be seen on the horizon, only the blue sky and smooth water. The isolation from the rest of the world was complete. As I watched the ship slide slowly and steadily through the water and everything seemed so peaceful and serene, a feeling of unreality would come over me. Was it really possible that Europe was in turmoil and the threat of brutal war hung heavily in the air?

There were among us plenty of people who were eager to organize and lead any activity they could think of. There were exercises every morning on the deck, walking or running the length of the ship, all kinds of games and best of all, dancing, which I loved. Maurice and I joined most of the activities, but we spent some time writing letters to our families and friends who we had left behind. We also liked to take our own private walk all over the ship, getting acquainted with the sailors, waiters, and engineers, and exploring all hidden places. We liked to watch the beautiful sunsets, admiring the richness of colors.

I will never forget the marvelous beauty of one particular sunrise that we observed through the porthole of our cabin very early one morning. The sun was just emerging on the horizon in such a glory of colors that it practically took our breath away. I never saw such a spectacular sunrise before or since that morning.

The ship was divided into two classes—First and Tourist. The division was strictly enforced. The passengers from the tourist class in which we were travelling were banned from the first class, while the first class passengers liked to visit us and join in our activities. I felt it was very unfair, and was angered one time in particular when we were not allowed to visit Bermuda, where we made a stop. Only passengers in first class were privileged to go down onto the land. We complained bitterly to the Captain, but to no avail.

One of the organized activities was more than just entertainment. Some South Americans offered to hold classes in Spanish to give us at least a taste of a language we were going to use from now on. Maurice and I attended the daily classes faithfully and they proved to be a great help to both of us.

The life on the ship went on quite smoothly on the surface, but of course not all was nice and happy in our little world. There were fights and quarrels, and all kinds of rumors circulated all over the ship. One incident especially shook me up. I lived a sheltered life in my parents' house; my parents' marriage was a model for me and I was quite naïve in many respects. As it happened, a husband found his wife with another man. He became so enraged that he dragged both of them to the deck and threatened to throw them overboard as we all watched in horror.

Slowly things settled down; however, this incident left a lasting effect. The mood was subdued and quiet. Our journey was coming to an end. We were approaching the shores of Cuba. The view from the ship was magnificent: the white houses, the palm trees, and the sight of the Morro Castle—the fortress in Havana harbor—all of it was very impressive. I was looking forward to our arrival at this beautiful island.

But before we even had a chance to disembark, we got a taste of dealing with greedy and corrupt Cuban officials, and all of our illusions about a good life were shattered, at least for a while.

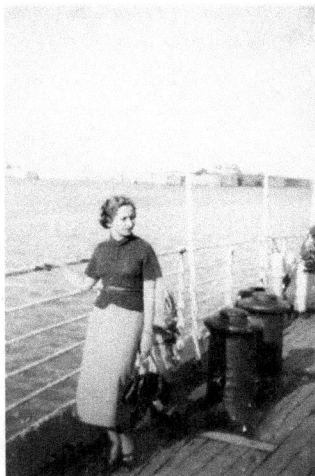

This picture was taken on board the Orduña, in December 1938 or January 1939, en route to Cuba. The fact that Ina is wearing lightweight clothing, although it was winter, suggests that they were nearing Cuba when the photo was taken. The buildings in the background might be Havana harbor.

For their first few months in Cuba, Ina and Maurice lived in relative comfort in Havana on a modest income that Maurice derived from an import-export business

that he established through connections in Poland. But that income stopped abruptly when Poland was invaded by the Nazis in September 1939.

San Antonio Del Rio Blanco

If anybody were to ask me today why we chose this little, sleepy town for our new venture, I would be at a loss to give any reasons or circumstances for this choice. All I remember is that we had to leave Havana, where we had lived for a while in relative comfort on a modest income from Polish connections that my husband had acquired before our departure from Europe. But this income stopped when Poland was invaded by the Nazis and all communication was abruptly cut off. Getting any kind of a job was out of the question; aliens were banned from all jobs. We were faced with yet another dilemma: what were we going to do?

After listening to a lot of contradictory ideas and advice, we finally decided to invest all of our remaining funds and some financial help from Maurice's uncle in the United States in a small variety store. Havana was much too expensive—it had to be a smaller town, but I still do not remember why we settled for San Antonio Del Rio Blanco!

But…there we were, with all our belongings piled up on the middle of a small, primitive cottage which we had rented for $20 a month. We were planning to divide it into our variety store and living quarters. What an ambitious plan!

San Antonio was a small, sleepy village about one hour by bus from Havana. To us, however, it seemed thousands of miles away from anything to which we were accustomed. We were really quite unprepared for this experience. There was not much happening in San Antonio, and the arrival of two strangers was a big event for the population of the village. Crowds of children as well as adults gathered around the truck that brought our possessions, inspecting every piece of furniture, bedding, and clothing, all the while pointing, screaming, and laughing. All of this commotion made us self-conscious, embarrassed, and uneasy.

Our first night in the cottage was a disaster. Nobody had warned us that in the country we needed mosquito nets over our beds, and we were attacked by clouds of mosquitoes hungry for "new blood." To add to our discomfort, a heavy tropical rain began to fall and the roof started to leak in a few places. We hunted for pots and buckets to save ourselves from the flood, and our belongings from damage. We were tired, angry, and discouraged.

We survived the disastrous night. The sun was shining the next morning, and our spirits rose. The people from the village turned out to be helpful and friendly. The roof was fixed. We acquired mosquito nets, and we set about to arrange our store and our home. We spoke fluent Spanish by that time, so there was no problem in communication. But people were so unbelievably curious that we might as well have been living in a glass house. There were forever people—not only children, but adults—peering into our windows and door, watching every step we made, practically looking into our cooking pots and tasting the food!

At first I was angered and annoyed by this intrusion into our privacy, but when I realized that there was no malice, but only childlike curiosity in the people's behavior, I relaxed and the whole situation began to amuse me. After a while, the people's curiosity was satisfied, the novelty of our being strangers wore off, and we were accepted as familiar figures: Maurico and Inez—the tenderos (shop keepers). We were part of village life.

What bothered us most, however, was the unbelievable ignorance and indifference of the people of San Antonio about the war, the Nazis, the Jews, and anything else beyond their immediate, small world. One incident is etched in my memory, never to forget. One day we were visited by a local missionary, who tried to sell us the New Testament (probably assuming we were pagans). In response, Maurice took out our Hebrew bible and showed it to the man, explaining to him that we were Jews, practicing the Jewish religion. The man listened attentively but when Maurice was finished, he turned and asked quite seriously, "Pero ustedes son Christianos, verdad?" ("But you are Christians, aren't you?") After this experience, we never started any discussions with the local people on serious subjects.

Life was not easy. Between the store and the primitive housekeeping, there was not much time for pleasure. But it really was not all that bad, either. A few better-educated families started to shop at our store and friendships developed. We spent many evenings over delicious Cuban coffee, relaxing and enjoying the company.

I particularly loved our night walks in the country. The air was incredibly clear and pure, filled with the intoxicating fragrance of a unique Cuban flower which blooms at night. It is called "Caballero de la Noche" (Night Gentleman). The sky was bright with a million stars I could not even see in the city, and I felt peaceful and almost happy.

But how could I forget that there was a war going on in Europe and people were dying? I did not have any news from my family in Poland and I feared the worst. We could not stay much longer isolated from the world; we had to change our life.

Just then we received word from the U.S. consulate that my quota number had come up and I was to receive an entry visa to the United States. But again the news was not entirely happy. Maurice was under a different quota and would still have to wait his turn. I had to go, because otherwise I would lose my turn. We hoped the separation would be just a few weeks, but it was the beginning of a miserable, most lonesome year for both of us.

Adios Cuba

It had been two and a half years since we had arrived in Cuba. The struggle to make a living was long and hard, and still we did not succeed in establishing ourselves in any way. Finally, we began to realize that this country was not meant for us.

I will always be thankful to my father for the thoughtful and wise advice he gave us as we were preparing to leave Poland for Cuba. He suggested that we register for immigration to the United States. We were lucky we did, for now we saw that this was our only hope of a better and more satisfying life.

So, when my long-awaited and long-hoped-for entry visa arrived, we should have been very happy. Instead, we were bitterly disappointed and confused. My husband's number had not come yet, and there were no indications of how long we would have to wait for his visa.

The reason for the delay was that, for purposes of immigration to the U.S., quota numbers we assigned according to birthplace rather than country of citizenship. I, of course, was under the Polish quota. But Maurice had been born in the small border town of Czernowitz, which had belonged to the Austro-Hungarian Empire at the time of his birth, but returned (or was given) to Romania after World War I. He was therefore considered under the Romanian quota, which was very small—approximately ten people per year. He was just an infant when his parents moved away from Czernowitz, but rules were rules, and nobody was willing to change them.

I was given three months to decide if I wanted to get an entry visa, and after that time I would lose my turn. All this time we argued endlessly. I refused to go to the

U.S. alone and leave my husband behind. Maurice was more practical. He argued that it would be unwise to lose my turn; besides, I could probably be of more help in the States than waiting together with him in Havana. He felt, also, that his entry visa would arrive soon, because very few people were able to leave wartime Europe. Finally, he convinced me. We waited until almost the last minute, all the time hoping that we could still leave Cuba together.

Finally, the day of departure arrived and there was no turning back. Very reluctantly and with a heavy heart, I boarded a ship in Havana on that bright day in March, 1941. I was going alone to fact another strange land and did not know what to expect. I hoped, of course, that our separation would be a short one and we would be together before long. But it did not turn out that way.

I have only a few, blurred memories of my arrival in the United States. The ship brought me to Miami, Florida, and from there I took a train to New York. My husband's brother Anselm met me at the train station. He, his wife, and her family were lucky to have arrived in the United States some time before.

I do not have any recollection of how or where I spent my first night and the following few days. But I remember very well that I started looking for work almost immediately after I arrived. The money I brought with me would not last for long. I found work in a decorative flower factory from 8:00am to 5:00pm for $15 a week.

There was no room for me in Anselm's household, so I stayed with Maurice's Uncle Joseph and Aunt Fanny Friedman in Brooklyn for a short while. But I treasured my independence, so as soon as I started working, I rented a room in the neighborhood for $4 a week and I was on my own.

My first impression of New York was very strange. It was the first time I had seen skyscrapers and such unbelievable crowds of people and cars. Yet I had an eerie feeling that I had seen it before, as if I were coming back home after a very long absence. I was working hard, unaccustomed as I was to factory tempo and routine. I had neither time nor money nor desire for entertainment, or even looking for friends. I did not have any relatives of my own, so I was happy that I was warmly accepted by Maurice's aunt and uncle and his American cousins.

Also, some of his old friends from Vienna, who were lucky enough to have escaped from Europe, were really nice to me. Everybody was very sympathetic about my problem and about my own family which had stayed behind in Poland. There was no news at all from my family for a long time, and what news came through from Europe was very distressing.

The time was passing by. All I could think of was Maurice alone in Havana, and I wondered if he was missing me as much as I was longing for him. We exchanged letters almost daily, but that was a poor substitute for being together. As I was working for my support in New York so was Maurice working in Havana. He was, however, in a more difficult situation, because as a foreigner he was not allowed to get a job. He became a travelling salesman, and as a result his health suffered. He was diabetic and had a hard time maintaining his diet and his routine. I was very worried. As we were waiting for Maurice's visa, the days became weeks, the weeks stretched into months, and still there was no news.

Then the blow! The Japanese bombed Pearl Harbor on December 7, 1941 and the U.S. was drawn into the war.

I realized what it meant to the people of the U.S. I saw it on the faces of people around me. Their sons, husbands, and brothers would be sent to the battlefields and maybe to death. My heart really ached for all the people and maybe I should have considered myself lucky that my husband was at least safe. But I was selfish and all I could think about was how this news would affect my personal life. And the news was really bad. It was announced that all immigration was to stop for the duration of the war.

I was crushed, and what was worse, there was nobody I could turn to for advice and reassurance. My husband's family and friends, who had been so nice to me, had all of a sudden turned ice cold. All the invitations stopped and even my telephone calls were cut short. I kept asking myself what I possibly could have done to bring about this change and to be so utterly abandoned. I was hurt and bewildered. Not until Maurice joined me did I learn the reason. Somebody was spreading malicious rumors about my being unfaithful to my husband which, of course, was a complete lie.

To add to my distress, Maurice became quite impatient and kept asking me in every letter to do something—anything—to get him out of Cuba. I was really alone, with no hope. Life seemed like a long, dark tunnel with no light at the end. Finally, I could not stand it any longer. I hated waiting, and this wait was the worst of them all. I just had to take some action. Without asking anybody, I decided to take a train to Washington and go to the Immigration Bureau and plead my case.

During the war, the State Department in Washington, D.C., was an armed camp, with armed guards at every door and a thorough check of everybody who wanted to enter the building. So I gathered all my courage and succeeded in being admitted into the building.

I was lucky! My interviewer in the Immigration Bureau was a pleasant young man who listened attentively to my sad story and showed real understanding of my situation. At the end of the interview, he said (and I will never forget those words), "I am afraid I cannot help you right now, but if you will send me a letter stating all the facts you just presented to me, I will see what I can do for you." Those simple words brought new hope into my life and restored my faith in humanity.

I rushed back to New York and immediately went to the Jewish Family Service. Together with a friendly and helpful social worker, I composed this important letter. I did not trust the mail. Once again I took the train to Washington, this time to deliver the precious letter personally to my young interviewer. Afterwards, there was nothing more for me to do but wait. At least this time I had some hope.

When I look back at this particular period of my life, I cannot believe that it was me who was so bold. I still wonder where I got the courage and strength. I was always shy and not too sure of myself, but I was so desperate and determined that I forgot my shyness.

As I waited for news, my mood alternated between hope and fear of disappointment. I waited for a miracle, and—unbelievably—it did happen! About three weeks after I delivered the letter in Washington, Maurice called me, hardly able to talk from excitement. He had his entry visa in his hands and was coming to join me in the U.S.A. All I could say was, "Thank God!" It was a miracle, and I helped it to happen.

As he had done in Vienna a few years earlier, Maurice went into business with his brother Anselm. His business card from that era reads: "Teich Hnos. [Hermanos = brothers] Representaciones y Comisiones Edificio Gomez, Dpto. 402 Morro 53, Habana Telefono A 5-0481

Part Three

A New Life in a New Country

And That Was the Last Time I Saw My Family

Together Again

How can I describe my feelings while I waited for the arrival of my husband after almost one year of separation? I was elated, happy, and anxious at the same time. It had been such a long time since we were together; I wondered if everything between us would be the same again.

I did everything I could to look my best. I had my hair done in the beauty parlor. I wore my best clothes. But I had lost a lot of weight and I was afraid I looked changed. I do not remember what kind of day it was when I was on my way to the railroad station. But for me, on this day, the sun was shining bright and the sky was beautiful and blue. I wished and hoped that I could be alone to greet Maurice. But his brother and his brother's wife were there already, so I knew that I would not have the privacy of my feelings, and I would have to share this moment with other people.

That is exactly what happened. My sister-in-law did not even give me the privilege of greeting my husband first, but quickly ran ahead as soon as he stepped out of the train. She embraced him even before I had a chance to come close to him.

Maurice had lost a lot of weight also and looked awfully thin to me. I immediately made a mental promise to take good care of him. I have very few memories of the days that followed Maurice's arrival in New York. We probably spent time with family and friends, but for me what we did was not really important, as long as we were together. Our "honeymoon," however, could not last forever; we had to face once more the problem of making a living.

Maurice was in a very optimistic mood and the future appeared pretty bright. The time he had spent in Cuba proved helpful in deciding what direction he intended to look for a way of supporting me and himself. A lot of people had come over to Cuba from Belgium in the last few months. They were in the diamond business and had a lot of connections in the United States. Maurice was given many names and addresses to contact in the diamond trade. There was, however, a problem. To become a diamond dealer one had to have capital, which we, of course, did not have. So Maurice settled for a diamond cutter's job. It was not what we wished for, but it was good for a beginning.

Through Maurice's connections, I also got a better-paying job. During the war a lot of small factories had sprung up, working for the armed forces. I worked in a knitting factory which manufactured woolen gloves for the army. Life settled into an everyday routine, and even the icy atmosphere of friends and family that had hurt me so badly while I was alone changed again, clearing up the puzzle of their attitude. The future, although modest and quiet, looked bright. And, what was best of all, I was expecting a baby!

But in the midst of all that optimism and happiness a great shadow hung over our minds. We still did not have any news about the family we had left behind in Europe. The way I learned of their fate, and the fate of six million other Jews, was traumatic. One day I came home early from work. I tried to relax and read the daily newspaper, which was supposed to be delivered in the morning. I could not find it anywhere. Finally I spotted it behind the armchair I was sitting on, and I immediately understood why it had been hidden from me.

Big black headlines proclaimed "Hitler's Plans to Exterminate the Whole Jewish Race." The articles that followed were even worse—describing the concentration camps, tortures, and gas chambers. Whenever I think about this moment, the helpless rage and horror still grip me just as they did so many years ago.

Maurice found me in tears. He told me the reason that he had hidden the newspaper was that he was afraid of my reaction and wanted to be with me at that moment. He tried to console me by saying firmly that no matter how much Hitler would try to proceed with his devilish plan, the Jewish people would survive. Still, it was not hard to figure out the fate of our families...

But life had to go on, and now we had not only our own lives to think about, but also the baby that was due to be born in a few months. We were very frugal and managed to save some money. We were just about to move to a small apartment from the rented room in which we had been living, when another change came into our lives. An old and good friend of my husband who was a diamond dealer made my husband an offer that was hard to refuse. It was to become his representative in Chicago. The offer came quite suddenly, and we knew it meant starting from scratch again, apart from the fact that the baby was due in two short months. It was a hard decision, but I knew that Maurice was a much better businessman than a diamond cutter, and the offer was very tempting. We quickly accepted, in spite of all our family and friends trying to talk us out of moving to Chicago. At least, people were saying, I should stay in New York until Maurice could arrange everything and the baby was born.

But I would not listen to any of these suggestions. My place was with my husband, and whatever was going to happen, we would not be separated again. It was not easy, to say the least. There were so many things to take care of—finding a place to live (we could not stay in a hotel for long), finding a doctor and a hospital. I still wonder how we managed all this in such a short time. In addition, Maurice had to find a place for himself in a business district, to start his work and establish himself.

When I think about it, Maurice was really wonderful and very resourceful. Through some acquaintances, we found a small one-bedroom apartment on a quiet little street—Hampden Court—on the north side of Chicago. After a few days in a hotel, we began to settle into the apartment, buying furniture and other household needs. I was trying to hurry and have the house ready before the baby was supposed to come. Then, one afternoon—I will never forget it—I was on a stepladder hanging curtains in our bedroom, when my baby gave me a signal. It was ready to face the world. Our son was born December 17, 1942, and all of a sudden the world was beautiful and a very happy place.

Bertie and Maurice, 1942

Ina and Maurice with Bertie, 1943

And That Was the Last Time I Saw My Family

Chicago

After our son was born, life settled into an everyday routine. Maurice left early each morning to go to his office downtown and attend to his business. I, of course, stayed home with the baby. The apartment in which we lived at that time was located on a very small, very quiet street and there were no young people around. Until that time, I never realized—in fact, never gave a thought to—what a deep change in people's lifestyle the arrival of a first baby would bring. Gone were the days or nights of freedom when we could go out at a moment's notice as we were accustomed to doing. Our time had to be carefully planned and all our activities adjusted to the baby's needs. It was winter time in Chicago, and freezing weather, and lots of snow kept me and the baby indoors most of the time.

Generally, I was happy and contented doing all of my household duties, and I especially loved to take care of the baby. But occasionally, I became restless and moody, feeling isolated and trapped in the tiny one-bedroom apartment without any outside outlet. We were strangers in Chicago, only just beginning to meet people and make friends, and there was no family around to give us help or relief.

Sometimes I felt sorry for myself and almost envied Maurice for his freedom of movement. But those moods did not last long. One look at my son's bright eyes and eager smile, and a feeling of gratitude would overwhelm me—the realization of the richness of my life after so many sad experiences. The thought of having my husband back after a long separation and the joy of having a baby was enough to make me guilty of feeling selfish, and I was happy again.

After a few months, we realized that our tiny apartment was really too small for comfort, and we started looking for a better place to live. We found a two-bedroom apartment on the opposite side of Chicago, the South Side, on Paxton Avenue. The apartment was very comfortable, sunny and pleasant. It had, however, one bad feature. It was located in a third-floor walkup. We realized that this meant more problems, carrying the baby, the carriage, and bags of groceries. But we had no choice—apartments were hard to find. And the location was wonderful: Jackson Park was just one block away, and a beautiful sandy beach on Lake Michigan was within a short walk.

Our building was full of babies and older children. Most of our neighbors were friendly and eager to help, as all of us were in the same situation. The park benches were always filled with children of all ages—babies in carriages and in strollers, toddlers forever running away and mothers and grandmothers chasing after them. It was a noisy, lively world, and I immediately and gratefully became part of it.

Maurice was a wonderful father, never too tired to play with the baby or take him for a stroll while I was trying to work or relax. He also liked to help me in the kitchen, but like most European men, he was more trouble than real help. How well I remember all those dirty dishes and pots and pans left for me to scrub after a Mother's Day "surprise" breakfast in bed! But I did not mind it; he loved me, and he tried his best, and I certainly appreciated his effort.

Like all new parents, we were fascinated with every phase of our bright little boy. His nickname was Bertie--as his full name, Albert, seemed too serious for a baby. He was also quite a character. He never learned to crawl on all fours as a baby was supposed to. His means of locomotion was unique—he propelled himself with his hands from a sitting position and arrived everywhere he wanted to go. He started to talk quite early and was growing into a handsome, healthy, and bright little boy. Maurice was doing quite well in his diamond business and for the first time in our married life, we felt comfortable and secure enough to enjoy life.

We met a lot of people and formed two separate sets of friends. One group was composed mostly of immigrants from Poland and we promptly organized a social club we called "Club Ezra." We met once a month and had a lot of fun. We also formed a circle of friends who were refugees from Austria and Germany. We became very friendly with a couple from Vienna, whose son Gerry was just two months older than our son. We spent a lot of weekends together and this friendship lasted for many years.

Our little boy was a pleasure to look at and a joy to be with. I should have been fulfilled and satisfied. But somehow I was not. I had a strange, disturbing feeling that I was missing something. Then I recognized the feeling—I did not want our son to be an only child. I wanted him to have a brother or sister. I wanted to have another baby!

Did I get my wish? Of course I did. This again is part of another story.

And That Was the Last Time I Saw My Family

Bertie and Ina on the balcony of the apartment on the South Side of Chicago, 1943

Bertie and Maurice in Jackson Park, Chicago, 1945

Judy Makes Her Appearance

Our son, Bertie, was only three and a half years old and we did not know if he understood all that my husband and I were trying to tell him. We held long conversations with him about the baby that would soon be coming to join our family. We tried to describe in glowing colors how nice it would be to have a playmate right here in our own house.

The thing that was hardest to explain was that we could not promise him a brother as he wanted; we vaguely mentioned that a sister would also be very nice to have. He was not very much concerned about the whole thing, but was very happy about the prospect of spending a few days at his best friend Gerry's house, while Mommy was to go to the hospital to get the baby.

It was all quite clear to him until I had to rush to the hospital unexpectedly with certain symptoms that proved to be a "false alarm." When we were coming home the same day from our friends' house, he was quite confused. He kept looking suspiciously at me and around me, looking for the baby, not saying anything, but his eyes were asking, "Where is the baby?"

It was a very hot day, that Sunday in August, which, after so many years, still remains clear in my memory. Our apartment had no air conditioning. The fans seemed to bring more hot air in, and we all were not feeling well, particularly myself. We decided to cool off by having lunch in a restaurant and going to a movie afterwards, then wait for the evening air to cool.

It was around 9:00pm when we returned home. After a light supper, we put our Bertie to bed. We finally sat down and tried to relax while listening to the news on the radio. All of a sudden a sharp pain went through my body and I knew immediately that it was time to go to the hospital. But this was not as simple and easy as it might appear. We lived on the South Side of Chicago, and my doctor practiced at Columbus Hospital, on the North Side, quite a distance from our house. We did not own a car, and neither did any of our friends.

Maurice started calling all the taxi companies, but with no success. Sunday night was a bad time to get a taxicab. At first I was not worried, hoping that somehow we would get a cab, but as the time passed, I became frightened, knowing for sure that the baby was on the way. Our next door neighbor, Mrs. Jones, hearing the commotion and our voices, came to our door. She also became worried. All of our phone calls were fruitless and we were all standing there looking at each other, totally at a loss as to what to do. Now we really were afraid that I would not reach the hospital in time. Finally, we had an idea—ask the police for help!

Maurice did not even have to explain the whole situation. Fifteen minutes later a police officer came to our door announcing that a (so-called, at the time) 'paddy wagon' was waiting downstairs to take me to the hospital. By now all our neighbors were awake and they all watched my descent from the third floor to the waiting police car. Bertie slept through the whole commotion: Maurice had to pick him up, wrap him in his pajamas in a blanket and carry him downstairs.

It was a strange experience and strange feeling, sitting the police 'paddy wagon'—me with a big belly, and Maurice with a child wrapped up in a blanket on his lap. People stopped in the street to stare at us. I wondered what went through their minds—they probably were thinking of us as criminals who had done something to the child. We stopped at our friends' house and left our son in their care as we had previously arranged.

But there was trouble again, as it turned out that the police car could not go out of its district to drive us all the way to the North Side. They stopped a cab that was on its way to pick up a customer and ordered the driver to take me and Maurice to the hospital. The cab driver realized immediately that it was an emergency and became very nervous and frightened that the baby might make its appearance in his cab. He started racing through the streets, weaving in and out of traffic, and his hand never left the horn.

We were sitting on the edge of our seats, holding our breath, expecting at any moment a crash and accident. With a great deal of luck, we finally arrived at the hospital, and we all sighed a sigh of relief. It was exactly midnight when we got there. The nurses were waiting outside with a wheelchair and my doctor was also there, all ready and waiting for me.

Now the frantic activities of preparation began in earnest. One hour later, the daughter I had wished for all the time was born. I was grateful and very, very happy.

A few days later, we came to our friends' house to pick up our son. The boys, Bertie and Gerry, were outside, most interested in the toys we promised as presents from the baby. Bertie acted strangely: he kept throwing curious glances at me and the bundle in a pink blanket on my lap, but he refused to even look at his little sister. It took some time before he finally accepted Judy and got used to the idea that she was here to stay and that he had to share his Daddy and Mommy with her.

My birthday is August 20. Judy was born one hour into August 19. Had she waited one more day, she would have given me the best birthday present I ever received in my life!

Bertie and Judy with Maurice, circa 1947

And That Was the Last Time I Saw My Family

All About Judy

When my daughter Judy was born, she was an ordinary newborn baby. Of course she was beautiful in my eyes, but I realized that a tiny, skinny baby with matchstick legs and arms, with skimpy hair of undetermined color, could not look beautiful to anybody but me.

Soon, however, in what seemed only a few short weeks, there was a complete metamorphosis. She grew a head of thick golden curls. Her little body filled out and her hazel eyes became bright and full of sparkle. She seemed to grow right before my eyes. She started to walk very early, before she was one year old, and pretty soon she was not only walking but running. It was such a pleasure to my eyes to see her plump little legs taking her anywhere she wanted to go.

At a very early age she showed an unusual wish for independence. When she fell down, she never cried, she pulled herself up, refusing all offers of help. She surprised me one day while I was feeding her by grabbing the spoon from my hand and starting to eat by herself. And from that day on, she always ate by herself.

She started to talk a little later than her brother, but, perhaps under his influence, she quickly began forming short sentences. Her first words, apart from the usual "Daddy" and "Mommy," were "cookies" and "shoes," (which she pronounced "snoos"). It may sound funny, but even now my daughter Judy is very fond of cookies. And shopping for new shoes is her favorite pastime—among more important interests, of course.

One experience from her early childhood, even after so many years, is still vivid in my mind and memory. When she was about one year old, she caught a cold, which somehow developed into a severe asthma attack. How well I remember carrying her in my arms all night long waiting for the doctor to come in the morning. I remember the feeling of panic and helplessness watching my baby fighting for every breath, too weak even to cry, and me not being able to do anything for her.

The doctor came early in the morning. He gave her a shot and prescribed medication. The crisis was over. She still had a few asthma attacks afterwards, but they were less severe and, being prepared, we were less panicky when they came.

Judy often used to stand by the window in the evening and watch the stars and especially the moon. I still have to laugh when I recall her running to me one evening, very agitated and distressed. "Mommy! Mommy! Come look!" she cried, "The moon is broken! There is only half of it in the sky. What is going to happen?"

She was a cheerful, happy child and wonderful company to me while her brother Bertie was at school. She seemed to enjoy being with me, because she refused to go to nursery school. The building we lived in at that time in Chicago was full of children of all ages. They quarreled and fought sometimes, but they also played well together. The favorite place for games and play was a nearby empty lot. The older kids usually did not admit younger kids to their games, but Judy was an exception. Though much younger, she could hold her own in games and disputes.

When Judy reached her fifth birthday, the time came to be enrolled in "real school"—O'Keeffe School on the South Side of Chicago, where Bertie attended the third grade. I promised Judy a present that she would get when I came to pick her up. I was a little apprehensive about her reaction to being left in school. She had never gone to nursery school, and was hardly ever separated from us. I was afraid she might resist, cry and cling to my skirt, like a lot of other youngsters. But not my Judy. When the time came to follow the teacher, she smiled, waved goodbye, and said, "See you later, Mommy."

I was left with a strange feeling of hurt and disappointment. Was it really so easy for my little daughter to leave her Mommy behind? Didn't she love me? I felt a sense of loss and, instead of going to the empty apartment, I walked around streets in the neighborhood until it was time to pick Judy up.

I did a lot of thinking during those few hours, about myself and Judy. Finally, I realized that the ease with which she left me was a sign of faith and trust in me. She knew I kept my promises and she never doubted that I would be there waiting for her after school. I remember how thrilled she was with the doll bassinette I bought for her for the first day of school.

When I look back at those days, nostalgia overcomes me. Those were good times. The children were young and very close to us. There were problems, also, but Maurice and I were young, and we were sure we could solve them. I know those times cannot come back again, but the memory of them will never fade away.

Judy, circa 1947

Take Her Back!

Maurice and I considered ourselves well-prepared for coping with sibling jealousies. We dutifully read many child psychology books recommended to us, as well as articles dealing with this problem. We also, of course, listened carefully to the advice of other parents who thought themselves experts on the subject. Still, anticipating some problems, we enrolled Bertie in a nursery school hoping that a few hours in the morning would give me time to take care of the baby and of myself. We enrolled him a couple of months before the baby was born, so he wouldn't blame the baby for being away from Mommy and from home.

Bertie loved the nursery school; he enjoyed the company of the other children and loved the songs and games. He looked forward every day to going to nursery school. We congratulated ourselves for such a good idea. Yes, we thought we were such wise parents…but our problem was different from all we had learned.

The trouble started right at the beginning, right after we brought the baby home. Bertie was very angry with me, did not want even to look at the baby, and once or twice I heard him mutter under his breath, "Take her back, I don't want her!" Of course, I ignored it. He also refused to go to nursery school and would not leave my side all day long.

Previously, he had been a cheerful, happy, and very cooperative child. Now he became sullen, rebellious, and defiant, and would not listen to me or Maurice when we tried to assure him that we loved him just as much as before and we always would love him. Maurice designated special times to spend exclusively with his son, and this probably helped in the long run. But in the meantime, the task of caring for the baby and my rebellious son became almost too much for me.

My ingenious son invented a game that almost drove me to a nervous breakdown. One day, I was just settling down with Judy in my arms and starting to nurse her. Bertie was always close by my side, but this time he suddenly and quietly left the room. The house was quiet and I was wondering what he was doing, hoping he had found something to amuse himself. (Television was unknown at that time.)

Suddenly, a loud noise and the sound of breaking glass came from the direction of the kitchen. I quickly put the baby in the crib. She, of course, started to protest at the top of her lungs. I raced to the kitchen, and there in the midst of pots and pans pulled out of all the kitchen drawers and cabinets, stood my son, with a triumphant smile on his pixie face, looking straight in my eyes and waiting for my reaction.

I really did not know what to do. I understood very well the reason for this behavior, but with all the reading and listening to advice, I was quite unprepared for this kind of call for attention. I knew, however, that it would be unwise to show anger or annoyance, because he was waiting just for that.

I took him by the hand, led him to his room, and told him firmly to stay there until I called for him. Then I rushed back to my howling daughter, finished nursing and put her, sleeping, in her crib. Then I went to the kitchen to pick up the posts and pans and put them back on the shelves and drawers and swept the broken dishes. Only after all that did I feel I was calm enough to speak to my son. I did not talk very much about what he had done, and I hoped that the episode was finished.

However, Bertie was not quite satisfied. He liked the game, and repeated it several times. I became too nervous to continue nursing the baby and I put her on the bottle and had a little more time to watch my son. After a while he got bored with staying at home and gladly went back to nursery school. I was very thankful for this relief, and less tired and less tense. I could handle Bertie better and give him more of my attention. The special time he had with his father also helped to convince him that things did not change for him. Finally, Bertie realized that his sister was here to stay; he took some interest in feeding and bathing her.

As they grew older, my son and daughter became very close and caring toward each other. They are now adults and lead different ways of life. I still feel, however, that some of this childhood closeness remains in their relationship.

Judy and Maurice, circa 1949

Where is My Baby?

There was one experience in my life that gave me a deep understanding of the feelings of grief and despair of families whose children are missing. It happened many years ago, but the memory of the incident is still vivid in my mind.

Our children were young: Albert was five years old, and my little daughter Judy was just about one-and-a-half. We were at the beach on Lake Michigan in Chicago, together with our good friends Friedl and Leo, whose son Gerry was also five years old and who, at the time, was my son's favorite playmate. The day was bright and sunny and very hot—one of those real lazy summer days when everything seems to slow down and nothing happens. Even our conversation was getting slow, and all we wanted to do was to just sit quietly or lie down and relax.

Albert and Gerry were playing by the water pump, splashing water at each other and having a wonderful time. My baby Judy was sitting nearby playing in the sand, busily sifting the golden sand from one little red pail to another. She seemed happy and satisfied. I kept a careful eye on the children, making sure that everything was all right. The picture in front of my eyes was beautiful: the cloudless blue sky, the sparkling water of the lake and the golden sand of the beach. The children were playing quietly and I felt peaceful and happy.

The next time I looked at the children, the boys were still playing at the water pump. At the place where Judy had been sitting a moment before, however, just a few steps away, the two little red pails were on the sand, but Judy was not there. My heart seemed to stop. I jumped to my feet and looked around, but she was nowhere to be seen. I yelled at the boys and asked them where Judy had gone. But, of course, they had not noticed anything. Albert started to cry. Now all of us were up on our feet, our tranquil mood all gone. We started looking for the baby in all directions, and asking everybody around if they had seen a small, blond, curly-haired little girl in a navy bathing suit wandering around. She couldn't have gone far, it was only a few minutes since I last saw her playing in the sand just steps away from me. Yet she was nowhere to be seen and nobody seemed to recall seeing a little girl all by herself.

Awful thoughts went through my mind: she was kidnapped, she had drowned in the lake, I would never see her again…The sense of guilt, fear, and despair was so powerful that none of us could think straight. But finally, Maurice started to reason. Our baby was not the first child that got lost at the beach, he kept repeating. We will find our baby, all we had to do is to take the proper steps.

The beach was very large and on this hot sunny day, it was overflowing with people. How could you find a little child who barely knew her name on this enormous beach full of indifferent people? We needed help. We ran to the beach office, told them our story, and gave them a description of our little girl. Immediately, the loudspeaker started calling for people's attention and asking everybody to be on the lookout for a wandering little girl.

There was nothing more to do but wait. We returned to our place on the beach and sat in gloom listening to the loudspeaker and waiting, waiting for a miracle. As the time passed so slowly, the despair in my heart grew worse and worse and the hope of finding Judy grew dimmer and dimmer. The boys were subdued and quiet. Albert huddled close to me and hugged me, trying to console me.

Then suddenly, I saw my friend Friedl jump up and start to run. She was the first one to notice a young woman carrying a crying baby, walking toward the beach office. She ran quickly toward the woman and I ran right after her. It was my baby, my little Judy, crying "Mommy! Mommy!" and stretching her little arms to me. I took her in my arms, kissed her, hugged her, and thought I would never be able to let go. The kind young woman had seen my little girl wandering aimlessly and crying and knew immediately what to do. I will be forever thankful to her.

Maurice was right, after all. We got our baby back, but I know in spite of his outward calm, he went through the same torture that I did. Thank God for the happy ending. But the memory of this experience, though it happened many years ago, still haunts me sometimes and makes me overly anxious and worried about my family. When I look back at this incident, I realize that it probably did not last more than one hour—but it was certainly the longest hour of my life.

And That Was the Last Time I Saw My Family

Judy, Ina, and Bertie in the courtyard of the apartment building, circa 1947

The Shortcut

It was one important spring when Maurice got his driver's license. He had never driven a car before, and passing his driver's test was quite an accomplishment for him. Shortly afterwards, we became the proud owners of a maroon Nash, several years old. It was hardly a luxury car, but for us it meant freedom: freedom of movement, freedom to go and visit places that until then we had not had a chance to see. We were excited and delighted. Even Judy, who was too young to understand what all this jubilation was about, seemed to join in the excitement.

Maurice practiced his driving skills on the streets of Chicago with the help of our neighbors and good friends, who sat beside him giving him practical and moral support. Pretty soon he began to feel competent, and started driving us to the sand dune beaches in Indiana and different spots of interest around Chicago.

Summer was approaching, and with it vacation time. We planned a longer vacation, and decided to go to the Black Hills of South Dakota. It was quite a distance from Chicago, at least 1500 miles, but the roads were good and everything was going alright. Alright, that is to say, until we came to the mountains, and the roads started to be much more difficult.

Maurice had never driven a car on a mountain road; all of his experience was on level ground. He surely had a lot to learn about mountain driving, and also about the car. We encountered a lot of trouble; our car was quite old and had a very weak motor, and more than once we would start going uphill and the car would threaten to roll down. With quite a bit of luck, we reached the State Game Lodge in the Black Hills. We had rented a small cottage, quite primitive, with outdoor "plumbing" and a woodburning stove which we used both for cooking and heating, when the nights got very cold. It was not a very luxurious accommodation and we were not used to this kind of primitive life.

But the beauty of nature compensated for the lack of comfort. The surroundings were truly beautiful. The hills were covered with forests so thick that they appeared almost black—which is where the name Black Hills came from. A little creek with crystal-clear water ran right by the side of our cottage, and the children had a lot of fun wading in it. Bert attempted to fish wish his brand-new fishing rod, but as far as I remember, he never had any success in catching fish.

By far the biggest attraction was a nearby horse stable, and all of us, even Judy, went horseback riding, first in a corral, later outside. The horses were quite gentle and trained to be slow, which was quite fine with us. After a while we were allowed to take the horses out of the corral and into the forest, accompanied by a stable boy, who knew his way around and also knew how to handle the horses if necessary. Horseback riding in the forest was an experience, and gave one a feeling that city people hardly ever get. Here, far away from the noise and hustle of everyday life in the city, the silence is soothing, and prompts one to speak in whispers rather than shout or talk loudly. The singing of birds, which gets lost in the city, fills the air and the quiet steps of the horses on the soft earth feels like being in a special world of peace and contentment.

Remembering my own childhood, when picking berries was a big part of any vacation in the country, I often took the children into the forest to pick blueberries or whatever we could find. We prepared our breakfast and lunch in our cottage, but for dinner we went to the lodge. We became friendly with several other families, and the children played together.

One day, Maurice suggested a trip to Rapid City, which was not too far from where we were staying. But my husband always liked to take a "shortcut" wherever we went, even if the so-called "shortcut" proved to be longer than the regular road. Well, this time also my husband gave in to his hobby by finding yet another way to get to Rapid City instead of a safe highway.

He made inquiries all around and got a lot of advice. One of the suggestions appealed to him. The road was several miles shorter than the highway, and it was supposed to be very scenic. Right from the start, I did not like the name of this road—the Horse Thief Trail—and I seriously objected, but to no avail. Maurice could be quite stubborn on occasion. He told me that he was assured the road was easy and safe. Of course it was easy and safe, for drivers experienced in driving in the mountains, who knew their way around.

Well, off we went to Rapid City, by way of the Horse Thief Trail. At first it was just a very narrow path in the forest, but the farther we went the steeper it became, and finally it was only a narrow opening between the trees. Roots were sticking out of the ground, making the car jump and veer out of control all the time, threatening to send the car flying down the mountain with all of us to our deaths.

I do not think I was ever so scared in my whole life and so absolutely sure that we could not come out alive. I looked at the children. Judy did not understand the danger, and was laughing and chattering. But Bert was old enough to see and understand what was going on. He was terrified; he huddled in the corner of the back seat, covered his eyes, and his breath was shallow and fast, telling how scared he was.

Luckily, Maurice, in spite of being scared himself, stayed relatively calm and I am sure this saved our lives. At last the "scenic" part of the Horse Thief Trail came to an end, and the rest of the road, although steep and narrow, was smooth, with no unpleasant surprises.

This was an experience which we have never forgotten. For many years we talked about the Horse Thief Trail, relived the danger and could even laugh about it. After a while, it became a family joke, and we recalled our adventure in the Black Hills when the going was hard and rough.

My husband learned a few lessons from our vacation in the mountains that summer. He also gained a lot of experience in driving, and when we came back home, he liked to say, "Driving in Chicago is child's play!

And That Was the Last Time I Saw My Family

Bertie, Maurice, and Judy on vacation in the Black Hills, South Dakota

www.ingramcontent.com/pod-product-compliance
Lightning Source LLC
Chambersburg PA
CBHW060310100426
42812CB00003B/722